XECUTIVE 2.0

XECUTIVE 2.0

X20

Human Leadership for the Digital Age

JOHN 'LEX' ROBINSON

Published by Best Seller Publishing®, St. Augustine, FL
Best Seller Publishing® is a registered trademark.
Printed in the United States of America.

ISBN: 978-1-966395-98-0

For more information, please write:
Best Seller Publishing®
1775 US-1 #1070
St. Augustine, FL 32084
or call 1 (626) 765-9750
Visit us online at: www.BestSellerPublishing.org

Advanced Praise For **Xecutive 2.0**

"Lex is one of the most talented people I've had the fortune to work with and learn from. His ability to innovate, communicate, and inspire others to take action is unmatched. He brings clarity to complexity—and moves people and organizations forward."

— Lauren Lamp,
VP, Customer Success & Support, RangeForce

"Lex is a gifted speaker, a clear communicator, and one of the rare security leaders who can hold a room while still encouraging dialogue. His content consistently sparks insight and action and he is a true professional I'm always glad to work with."

— Scott Renna,
Cybersecurity Sales Executive

"Wise, self-motivated, and multi-skilled, Lex brings analytical precision and outside-the-box thinking to every challenge. A proactive expert and natural leader, I highly recommend his work."

— Mark Bernardin,
Customer Success Manager

"In over 20 years, I've worked with hundreds of project managers. Lex is in a class of his own. His leadership, calm decision-making, and ability to align diverse stakeholders drove enterprise-wide transformation in the face of resistance. He sets the standard."

— John Huston,
Former CIO/CTO/COO, Enterprise Transformation Leader

"Lex motivates teams and executes strategy with purpose. I've seen him guide projects that reshaped organizational direction and delivered tangible results. His ability to lead, adapt, and deliver is second to none."

— Dave Bradley,
M.S. Eng Mgt, PMP, IT Strategy & Profit Mentor

"Lex is a respected leader who blends energy, focus, and strategic clarity. His level-headed, fact-driven approach to problem solving is what sets him apart and what earns him the respect of those around him."

— Eric Mahaffey,
Principal Solution Architect, Lumen Technologies

To the builders of yesterday—the engineers, technologists, and
quiet operators who shaped the systems we now stand upon.

And to the leaders of today and tomorrow—those
with the courage to evolve, to speak truth, and
to lead with both vision and integrity.

You've built the future. Now it's time to lead it.

This book is for you.

Disclaimer & Advisory Note

The information provided in this book is for educational and informational purposes only. It is not intended as medical, psychological, or professional advice. Readers should consult with qualified professionals for advice specific to their personal circumstances, including medical conditions, mental health, or workplace challenges. The strategies, examples, and techniques shared are based on the author's research, personal experience, and work with clients, and outcomes may vary for individuals.

Table of Contents

A Manifesto for Human Flourishing

Technology is evolving faster than ever, and the true challenge isn't in its rise, it's in how we choose to wield it. The future of work, leadership, and human progress hinges on a simple truth: technology should empower, not overpower, our potential.

As leaders, we are at the forefront of this transformation. The choices we make today will shape tomorrow. We have the responsibility—and the opportunity—to guide this evolution, ensuring that it serves human flourishing and the greater good.

We are the architects of this future, committed to leadership that prioritizes people, purpose, and innovation. This is not about turning away from technology but about integrating it with wisdom and care to elevate what makes us human.

By undertaking this mission, we will:

- **Reclaim our humanity:** Lead with empathy, emotional intelligence, and authentic human connection at the core of our decisions.
- **Harness technology to amplify, not replace:** Use technology as a tool to elevate human capabilities, ensuring it enhances, not diminishes, the richness of the human experience.

- **Cultivate critical thinking:** Lead with clarity and purpose, questioning the status quo, challenging assumptions, and always seeking truth in a world of constant change.
- **Inspire innovation:** Foster creativity and bold thinking that inspires solutions which are both groundbreaking and deeply aligned with human needs and values.
- **Uphold integrity:** Champion ethical leadership, with transparency, honesty, and accountability as the pillars of our actions.

Leadership is the force that steers the course of our future, and with it, we have the power to shape a world where human potential is limitless. We are the leaders who will ensure that technology enriches lives, fosters flourishing, and upholds the highest standards of humanity.

Are you ready to lead with us?

From manifesto to movement—what's next is yours to claim.

Answer the Call, Step into the Movement

Unlock your reader bonus and join a leadership community built for transformation.

Welcome to the rebellion—where leadership meets purpose, and potential becomes performance. As a reader of Xecutive 2.0, you're not just here to absorb ideas. You're here to live them.

You've already taken the first step by picking up this book. What happens next might surprise you—because once you step inside, the shift from insight to action tends to happen faster than most expect.

What You'll Discover Inside the Xecutive 2.0 Community:

Exclusive Frameworks in Action - Go beyond the page with tools and strategies built to accelerate real-world leadership.

A Tribe of Growth-Oriented Leaders - Collaborate with high-performers committed to human-first leadership, innovation, and impact.

Leadership Challenges & Labs - Test your ideas, get feedback, and sharpen your decision-making, resilience, and influence.

Performance-Boosting Habits - Build rituals that drive energy, clarity, and execution—so you show up as your best self, every day.

Activate Your Reader Bonus

As a thank you for reading *Xecutive 2.0*, you're invited to claim **25% off Your First Month** in the Xecutive 2.0 Community.

This is your private gateway from reading to rising—where your leadership evolution begins to unfold before you even step inside.

Scan the QR code below to unlock your reader-exclusive reward.

Use code: X2UNLOCK at checkout.

Don't just read about leadership—live it.

I'll see you inside,

John 'Lex' Robinson
Lead | Empower | Xecute

Part I:

The New Era of Leadership

Where human potential meets exponential innovation.

This section lays the foundation for what it means to lead in the digital age. As the pace of change accelerates, the call for human-centered leadership grows louder. We'll dismantle the outdated myths, define the qualities essential for the future, and introduce the transformation that starts with self-awareness and vision.

The Human Leader in the Digital Age

The old leadership playbooks are breaking down. What once worked in stable boardrooms and predictable markets now crumbles under the weight of automation, complexity, and constant disruption.

Today's executive can't rely on legacy thinking or linear plans. They need clarity under pressure, the emotional intelligence to lead real humans through uncertainty, and the courage to grow while others freeze.

This isn't merely a fight to stay relevant; it's a call to reimagine leadership—where human insight, not just operational efficiency, drives the future.

Throughout my career, I've had the privilege of leading corporate teams, mentoring aspiring executives, and collaborating with some of the most talented technologists in the industry. My path has taken me to conferences, keynote stages, and training rooms, where I've connected with leaders striving to grow, adapt, and thrive.

These face-to-face interactions have allowed me to hear the triumphs, struggles, and aspirations of countless professionals who have followed my work or sought my guidance.

What has struck me most during these interactions, what I've found truly humbling, is how many remarkable individuals, despite their intelligence and achievements, have expressed feeling stuck, overwhelmed, or uncertain about their next steps. These weren't inexperienced executives or individuals lacking ambition. Many were seasoned professionals with years of expertise and notable accomplishments.

Yet, across all these conversations, familiar challenges surfaced: the struggle to find clarity in decision-making, the difficulty of maintaining the energy to lead effectively, and the constant pressure of keeping pace with the relentless speed of change.

These recurring insights left me with an undeniable realization: the traditional approaches to leadership development—centered on sharing ideas, frameworks, and best practices—are no longer enough. Leaders today need more than knowledge. They need tools and strategies to break through barriers, redefine their approach, and adopt a model of administration designed for the future.

We are living in a time of extraordinary possibility. Rapid advancements in Artificial Intelligence, automation, and engineering science are rewriting the rules. The strategies that once ensured success are no longer sufficient. Thriving in today's environment requires an integrated approach; one that sharpens the mind, strengthens the body, and leverages technology responsibly and ethically.

This book is your roadmap to navigating this new reality. It's a guide to becoming the leader the future demands, with tools and strategies to:

- Cultivate mental clarity and resilience to face uncertainty.
- Build physical vitality and focus to sustain high performance.
- Lead with empathy, decisiveness, and purpose.
- Adopt AI and digital tools as amplifiers of your impact, not threats.

Through practical tools, reflective exercises, and transformative stories, you'll uncover how to unlock your full potential and inspire those you lead. These insights are grounded in real-world challenges and opportunities, offering you strategies to navigate the ever-evolving demands of life and work.

Leadership isn't about having all the answers or achieving perfection. It's about growth, progress, and the courage to adapt.

My promise to you is this:

If you show up and engage fully with the ideas and strategies in this book, you'll walk away with the clarity, confidence, and capacity to lead at a level you may not have thought possible.

So, before you begin, ask yourself:

**What kind of leader do you want
to become in this new era?**

How to Approach This Book and Its Materials

Welcome to Xecutive 2.0. This book is not merely a guide, it's a roadmap to a game-changing process, one that will elevate your skills, sharpen your focus, and align your work with your most ambitious goals. To get the most out of these materials, here's how I suggest you approach them:

Read Through the Entire Book First

Before diving into implementation, read the book from start to finish. Doing so will give you a complete understanding of the concepts, frameworks, and strategies outlined in the Xecutive 2.0 program. Think of this first read as orienting yourself to the terrain. It's about seeing the big picture before you take your first steps. Understand the 90-Day Plan

At the conclusion of the book, you'll find a comprehensive 90-day plan designed to guide you through a structured approach to change. This plan is where all the pieces come together, and it's your blueprint to putting the ideas in this book into action. However, it's important to remember that change takes time, and this book, like the plan, is not about overnight change. It's about sustained, intentional progress.

Focus on What Resonates Most

As you read each chapter, take note of the ideas, strategies, or action plans that stand out to you. These moments of resonance are a signal. They point to the areas where you're ready to grow or where you'll see the greatest immediate impact. You don't need to implement every suggestion at once. Instead, pick one or two key takeaways from each chapter and focus on integrating those into your work and life.

Start Small, Build Big

Change doesn't happen in a single leap—it's a series of small, deliberate steps. Start with changes that you know you can succeed in implementing. Small wins build momentum, and over time, these incremental improvements will lead to meaningful growth. Give yourself the space and grace to grow at your own pace.

Revisit and Refine

This book is a resource you'll come back to often. As you implement ideas and experience progress, revisit chapters to deepen your understanding or to tackle new areas of growth. Each time you return, you'll find new insights or strategies that align with where you are in your life.

Embrace the Long-Term

Remember, Xecutive 2.0 is about a shift that unfolds over time. This isn't a quick fix or a one-size-fits-all solution. It's a process of evolving into the best version of yourself, both as a leader and as a human being. With intentional steps, a focus on what truly matters, and steady momentum, you'll build lasting change that fuels your professional success and personal fulfillment.

Approach this book with curiosity, patience, and a commitment to your own growth. The course ahead is life changing, and by engaging with these materials thoughtfully, you're taking the first steps toward becoming your own version of Xecutive 2.0.

The Leadership Evolution

The pace of change has shifted from incremental to exponential. What once was a steady evolution is now a constant disruption. Emerging technologies, global instability, and evolving cultural expectations have created a level of complexity that old models of command and control simply can't handle.

For now—and the foreseeable future—success won't be defined by how loudly someone speaks, but by how clearly they think, how deeply they connect, and how effectively they adapt. Authority no longer guarantees impact. Human intelligence, creative problem-solving, and emotional depth will.

This isn't a nice-to-have evolution. It's a requirement. To lead in today's world, we need an integrated approach—one that aligns mental clarity, physical energy, and the strategic use of technology to amplify our humanity, not replace it.

As I've experienced in my own career, success requires more than just technical expertise. It demands a new mindset, a new way of thinking, communicating, and leading. Only when I understood the importance of balancing clarity of thought, physical health and technological mastery did I start to see real gains.

I've witnessed this in my clients as well. Johnny, a consulting client, shared, "With training and coaching, I honed my current skills and habits while developing more clarity and focus on what my objectives are. Visions which I thought were clear have become even more vivid."

Johnny has learned that "to go fast, sometimes we must step back, focus in, and go slow, one small objective at a time." By focusing on small, intentional steps, Johnny found laser-sharp clarity, not just for himself but also in leading others. "The skills and habits I've been learning are not only paying off dividends in my own life but have improved my leadership of others."

Similarly, Mark found not only a calm sense of clarity in his goals but also improved his physical health and team dynamics. "Over the first ten weeks, I've found increased clarity on my most important goals and what it takes to achieve them. I've gained a real sense of calm from the process. As a result, there have been improvements in all areas of my life."

Mark realized that it wasn't about new techniques but about being more himself, a more balanced and confident leader.

One of the most powerful shifts I've seen came from Jeff. He came to me with a vision for his new business venture, prepared to accept a six-figure salary and 10% equity. But after gaining clarity on his purpose, he aligned his vision with his investors, creating excitement around the larger goal.

The result? "They offered me double what I really wanted; a multiple six figure salary and 15% equity. Implementing the framework helped me take a good achievement and make it something I didn't think was possible."

This book is designed to guide you. It's about equipping you with the tools to lead with vision, balance, and resilience in today's world.

By embracing an integrated approach, you'll be able to drive meaningful impact, and not just survive but thrive in this digital age. The future of leadership is about leading yourself first, and then inspiring others to do the same.

An Overview of Leadership Transformation

Acknowledge the Need for Change: Recognize that traditional management models may not be sufficient in today's dynamic environment.

Embody Leadership Holistically: Accept the need to integrate mental clarity, physical vitality, and the strategic use of technology for effective leadership.

Self-Reflect: Introspect on your current leadership style and identify areas for improvement.

Clarify Your Vision: Define your desired future state as a leader. What impact do you want to make? What kind of leader do you aspire to be?

Identify Strengths and Weaknesses: Analyze your existing strengths and weaknesses as a leader. What are your areas of expertise? Where do you need to develop further?

Shift Your Mindset: Cultivate a growth mindset, embracing continuous learning and adaptability. Be open to new ideas and approaches.

Develop Emotional Intelligence: Enhance your self-awareness, empathy, and emotional regulation skills.

Prioritize Physical and Mental Well-Being: Focus on maintaining a healthy lifestyle through regular exercise, sufficient sleep, and stress management techniques.

Adopt Technology Strategically: Explore and leverage innovative tools to enhance your leadership effectiveness (e.g., communication platforms, project management tools, AI assistants).

Continuous Learning: Engage in ongoing professional development activities, such as reading, attending workshops, and seeking mentorship.

The Five Pillars of Leadership for the Digital Age

You can't lead today with yesterday's mindset. The rules have changed. Complexity is no longer a challenge to manage—it's the environment we operate in.

Uncertainty isn't the exception—it's the baseline. Problems are layered, fast-moving, and often beyond the scope of traditional thinking. To lead effectively now, we must go beyond strategy and skills—we need self-awareness, team intelligence, and the ability to partner with technology, not be ruled by it.

Next-generation executives will thrive by mastering five core capacities: a clear, focused mind; a strong, energized body; powerful communication; adaptive creativity; and a principled approach to AI. Together, these pillars form the foundation of modern executive presence—one built not just for speed, but for sustained impact.

Clarity of Mind

The mental demands of leadership today require focus, strategic thinking, and resilience. Those who develop clarity of mind can develop more explicit goals and make confident decisions even in times of uncertainty. As Johnny put it, "Visions which I thought were clear have become even more vivid." It's about more than speed; it's also about precision. Leaders who master mental clarity can anticipate challenges, focus on what truly matters, and inspire their teams to take decisive action.

Physical Vitality

The fast pace and high stakes of the modern era require stamina, energy, and balance. Leaders who prioritize their physical health can handle stress better, sustain high performance, and inspire their teams. Mark's experience exemplifies this: "My blood pressure is down 20 points, and my staff is performing at a higher level than ever before." By focusing on personal well-being, Mark not only improved his own health but also elevated his team's effectiveness.

Communication Excellence

Communication is at the heart of effective orchestration. Whether it's inspiring your team, navigating conflict, or providing constructive feedback, how you communicate defines your success. Leaders who excel in communication understand the nuances of their audience and tailor their messages to resonate deeply. As John shared, "Learning to dream big with (clearly communicated) calculated steps has been one of the most impactful tools I've learned from this." Clear communication helps build trust, foster alignment, and empower teams to act. It's through this mastery that we move beyond simply managing and truly lead with purpose.

Creative Problem-Solving

In the face of ever-evolving challenges, leaders must be able to think creatively and approach problems from new angles. Those who excel in creative problem-solving can break through conventional barriers, find innovative solutions, and guide their teams through uncertainty. This skill is essential for navigating today's fast-changing world. As a client of mine once explained, "When I learned to tackle problems with a fresh perspective, I started seeing solutions I never would have before." The ability to think outside the box allows us to stay ahead of the curve and keep our teams engaged in finding the best possible outcomes.

Ethical Integration of AI Solutions

The rise of Artificial Intelligence presents both incredible opportunities and ethical dilemmas. Leaders must not only understand the capabilities of these tools but also integrate them responsibly. Ethical AI integration will drive innovation while ensuring transparency, trust, and accountability. It's about developing solutions that amplify human capabilities, not replace them.

Be the Change, Lead the Charge

The future requires us to embrace an integrated approach—one that balances the mind, body, and machine. When you integrate these elements, you'll develop the adaptability, foresight, and resilience needed to navigate the challenges ahead. The world needs leaders who are not just technically competent but who inspire others through clarity, health, responsible innovation, and creative solutions.

Leadership today doesn't require superpowers—but it demands authenticity and wholeness. To thrive, we must be forward-thinking, adaptable, and deeply rooted in our values and our teams. Embrace this, and you won't just keep up—you'll shape what's next and empower others to rise with you.

Debunking Leadership Myths

As we begin exploring the future state of executive leadership, we must challenge some of the long-held myths about what it means to lead. Too often, these misconceptions hinder the development of aspiring leaders and prevent organizations from unlocking their full potential. The following separates fact from fiction, helping you prepare for breakthrough future-ready leadership. Understanding and embracing these truths will empower you to adapt to the complexities of the modern world, set a clear course for your team, and lead with clarity, vision, and purpose.

Myth: Leaders Are Born, Not Made.
Fact: Leadership is Learned, Practiced, and Refined Over Time.

Many people believe that great leaders are born with innate qualities like charisma or decisiveness. In reality, these are skills that can be nurtured over time. With deliberate practice, learning, and feedback, anyone can improve their ability to lead. The true essence of leadership lies in continuous self-reflection, learning from experiences, and refining your abilities to adapt to different situations.

Myth: Leaders Should Have All the Answers.
Fact: Great Leaders Accept Uncertainty and Leverage Collective Expertise.

The expectation that leaders must always have answers can lead to decision-making paralysis and prevent teams from contributing their insights. Effective leaders are comfortable with ambiguity, relying on their teams to provide diverse perspectives. They create an environment where collaboration and expert advice are sought to solve difficult problems, demonstrating that leadership is not about having all the answers but about asking the right questions.

Myth: Leaders Must Always Be in Control.
Fact: Empowering Others Strengthens Leadership and Team Performance.

While it's tempting to believe that strong leadership means maintaining control at all times, true leadership is about empowering others. By trusting your team, delegating tasks, and fostering autonomy, you unlock creativity and enable ownership. This leads to higher morale, better decision-making, and an environment of collaboration where everyone thrives.

Myth: Command and Control Drives the Best Results.
Fact: Inspiring and Empowering Others Creates Stronger, More Adaptive Teams.

The traditional "command and control" style has become less effective in today's fast-paced, collaborative environment. Instead, a redefined style—focused on inspiring, motivating, and empowering others—drives higher engagement and innovation. Leaders who embrace this style create a shared sense of purpose and cultivate a culture of growth, resulting in more successful and agile teams.

Myth: Leadership Requires Distance and Detachment.
Fact: True Leadership is Built on Connection, Trust, and Direct Engagement.

The old-school placed executives on an organizational pedestal—separate from those they lead. But the reality is that leadership isn't about being above; it's about being among. The best leaders foster trust, alignment, and motivation through direct engagement, clear communication, and active listening. It isn't about keeping people at arm's length; it's about showing up, being present, and demonstrating that you are in it with them. A disconnected leader breeds disengagement. A connected leader builds a team that is committed, empowered, and aligned with the mission.

Myth: Micromanagement Drives Results.
Fact: Excessive Control Stifles Growth, Kills Creativity, and Demotivates Teams.

Micromanagement may appear to be an efficient way to control outcomes, but it limits the potency of both the leader and their team. By stepping back and trusting your team members to handle responsibilities, you allow them to develop their skills, increase job satisfaction, and contribute more creatively to the success of the organization. Leadership is about inspiring confidence, not controlling every action.

Myth: Leaders Must Always Be Tough.
Fact: Empathy and Vulnerability Strengthen Leadership and Team Trust.

The traditional image of leadership often revolves around toughness and assertiveness, but effective leaders also model empathy and vulnerability. These qualities are crucial for understanding and supporting your team. Leaders who show compassion foster trust and loyalty, while those who are open about their own challenges create a culture where vulnerability is seen as a strength rather than a weakness.

Myth: Leadership is a Solo Effort.
Fact: Great Leaders Build, Empower, and Rely on Their Teams.

Leadership is rarely a solitary pursuit. The most successful leaders surround themselves with strong, diverse teams and encourage collaboration. By recognizing and utilizing the unique strengths of each team member, leaders create a collective force that drives the organization forward. Enabling its members to thrive in an environment of cooperation, not isolation.

Myth: Digital Transformation is a Distraction.
Fact: Embracing Technology is Essential for Innovation and Leadership.

In the modern business world, digital transformation is anything but a distraction, it's a necessity. Leaders who fail to take advantage of technology risk falling behind. By leveraging tools and platforms that enhance communication, collaboration, and decision-making, leaders not only stay connected with their teams but also position their organizations to innovate and remain competitive.

Myth: Leadership is a Career Destination.
Fact: Leadership is a Lifelong Journey of Growth and Adaptation.

Leadership is not a destination but a mindset. True leaders understand that their growth is never complete. They seek opportunities for learning, adapt to changing environments, and strive for ongoing improvement. This mindset helps them stay relevant and effective, guiding their teams through today's business landscape and preparing them for the challenges of tomorrow.

By debunking these myths and embracing the truth behind them, you are now better equipped to make the shift necessary for effective leadership in the future. Remember, the shift involves a change in how you lead with clarity of mind, physical vitality, communication excellence, and the ethical integration of advanced technologies. As we move forward, we'll dive deeper into practical strategies for developing these elements.

Leadership Myths Busted: Facts for the Modern Leader

Myth: Leaders Are Born, Not Made.
Fact: Leadership is Learned, Practiced, and Refined Over Time.

Myth: Leaders Should Have All the Answers.
Fact: Great Leaders Accept Uncertainty and Leverage Collective Expertise.

Myth: Leaders Must Always Be in Control.
Fact: Empowering Others Strengthens Leadership and Team Performance.

Myth: Command and Control Drives the Best Results.
Fact: Inspiring and Empowering Others Creates Stronger, More Adaptive Teams.

Myth: Leadership Requires Distance and Detachment.
Fact: True Leadership is Built on Connection, Trust, and Direct Engagement.

Myth: Micromanagement Drives Results.
Fact: Excessive Control Stifles Growth, Kills Creativity, and Demotivates Teams.

Myth: Leaders Must Always Be Tough.
Fact: Empathy and Vulnerability Strengthen Leadership and Team Trust.

Myth: Leadership is a Solo Effort.
Fact: Great Leaders Build, Empower, and Rely on Their Teams.

Myth: Digital Transformation is a Distraction.
Fact: Embracing Technology is Essential for Innovation and Leadership.

Myth: Leadership is a Career Destination.
Fact: Leadership is a Mindset of Growth and Adaptation.

A Leadership Journey in the Digital Age: David's Wake-Up Call

The following story serves as a representation of the struggles executives face in today's fast-paced, technology-driven world. It highlights the need for a novel approach—one that blends traditional business strategy with mental, physical, and emotional resilience. While David's experience is fictional, it echoes the challenges and opportunities many leaders encounter as they navigate the digital age.

David had always prided himself on being a results-driven executive. For over 20 years, he had climbed the corporate ladder, building a reputation for his sharp strategic mind and ability to make tough decisions under pressure. As CEO of a mid-sized tech company, he had seen impressive growth, largely due to his relentless drive and singular focus on results. But lately, something has changed. The challenges his organization faced seemed more elaborate, and the demands on his time and energy were reaching a boiling point.

David had always relied on traditional methods—top-down decision-making, delegating tasks, and trusting his expertise to guide the company's direction. But as his company grew and the landscape shifted, the old ways no longer seemed to work. The demands for faster innovation, greater agility, and more collaborative problem-solving were becoming overwhelming. His team, once a well-oiled machine, seemed less engaged, and morale was starting to slip. His own stress levels were through the roof, and the constant decision fatigue was taking a toll on his health.

It wasn't until a series of setbacks—failed product launches, a tense board meeting, and a key team member leaving—that David finally took a step back. He realized that if he didn't change the way he led, his company would struggle to stay relevant in an increasingly competitive world.

His wake-up call came during a rare moment of reflection. While on a business trip to Silicon Valley, he had the opportunity to sit down with Elena, an executive in the tech industry whom he greatly respected. Elena had built a successful, innovative company while maintaining a sense of balance and authenticity. She had a reputation for fostering creativity, empowering her teams, and leading with a sense of purpose, rather than focusing solely on profit margins.

"What's your secret?" David asked her over coffee. "How do you stay ahead of the curve without burning out?"

Elena smiled knowingly. "It's no longer about working harder. It's about working smarter, and that means focusing on more than just business strategy. You must be able to lead yourself before you can lead others. In today's world, leadership requires an integrated approach. You need mental clarity, physical resilience, emotional intelligence, and a deep understanding of how technology and ethics intersect."

David was intrigued. It sounded too simple to be true, yet something about Elena's words struck a chord deep within him. He began to realize that his relentless drive had led him to neglect the very tools that would make him a more effective leader: his health, his mental clarity, and his ability to connect with his team on a deeper level.

The next few months were a period of meaningful change. He began to take on a more comprehensive approach, one that addressed not just his strategic mindset but also his physical, emotional, and cognitive well-being.

First, he focused on his mind. He began incorporating mindfulness practices into his daily routine, starting with just 10 minutes of meditation each morning. This simple practice helped him center himself and reduce the constant noise in his head. Soon, he noticed a difference in his ability to make decisions—he was clearer, more focused, and less reactive.

Next, David turned his attention to his body. He had neglected his physical health for years, relying on caffeine and late nights to fuel his work. He started exercising regularly, focusing on cardio and strength training to boost his energy levels. He also revamped his diet, opting for more nutrient-dense meals that fueled both his body and his brain. The results were immediate. He felt more energized, slept better, and had more stamina throughout the day.

But perhaps the most significant shift came in his executive presence. David realized that leading with authority alone was no longer effective. To truly inspire his team, he needed to lead with empathy and emotional intelligence. He began engaging with his team more openly, listening actively, and fostering an environment of trust and collaboration. Instead of dictating solutions, he started encouraging his team to contribute ideas, creating a more dynamic and innovative atmosphere.

As he made these changes, David's perspective evolved. He understood now that true success as a leader wasn't about being the smartest person in the room or always having the answers. It was about creating an environment where people could thrive, where they felt heard and empowered. It was about leading with integrity and authenticity, balancing the demands of the business with the well-being of those around him.

Within a year, David's company had turned a corner. His team was more engaged, productivity had increased, the culture was stronger, and the innovation pipeline had never been more robust. David had found his balance—not only in the results his company achieved but in the way he led. By aligning his mind, body, and inner drive, he became the kind of leader the future demands—resilient, high-impact, and purpose-led.

David's success wasn't just about personal reinvention; it was about recognizing the need for a new way forward. He realized that to succeed in a chaotic world, leaders must grow and care for every aspect of themselves, not just their strategy. This new paradigm—anchored in balance and integration—defines the future of leadership.

You've just seen how one leader redefined his impact by shifting how he thinks, moves, and leads. Imagine what might happen when you apply the same precision to your own performance. Let's start with your most valuable asset—your mind.

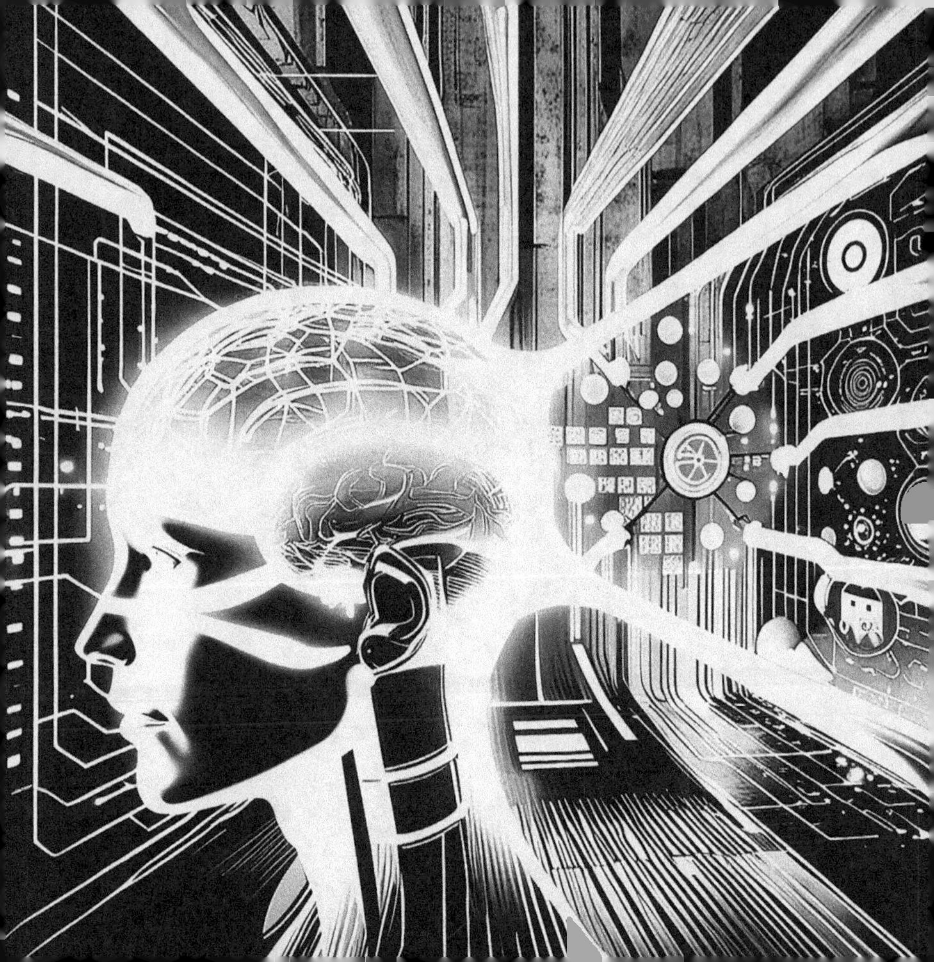

Part II:

The Cognitive Edge

Sharpen your mind. Clarify your priorities. Elevate your impact.

To lead effectively in high-stakes environments, your cognitive capacity must become a competitive advantage. This section equips you with tools to enhance focus, decision-making, and emotional intelligence—turning your mind into your most powerful leadership asset.

Cognitive Enhancement Strategies: Think Sharper. Lead Smarter

Ever walked into a high-stakes meeting and blanked on a critical detail? Felt your focus slip just when you needed razor-sharp clarity? Leadership isn't just about experience, it's about having your mind conditioned for focus, speed, and insight.

You're already juggling countless decisions, conversations, and challenges every day. But if your memory slips, your focus drifts, or your emotions take the wheel, your performance takes a hit. The most effective leaders don't just push harder—they train their minds to operate at a higher level.

These strategies will give you the mental edge to stay sharp under pressure, think strategically, and lead with confidence. Ignore them, and you'll keep feeling overwhelmed, reactive, and stretched too thin. Master them, and you'll take control of your mental state—and your future.

Memory: Strengthening Retention and Recall

Memory isn't just a tool—it's a foundational component of career success. If you forget critical details, you risk making weak decisions, missing opportunities, and losing trust. Your brain's ability to retain and recall vital information depends on two key systems:

Short-Term Memory – The hippocampus processes incoming information, but in a fast-paced, high-pressure environment, it gets overloaded quickly.

Long-Term Memory – This is where leadership power lies—storing and retrieving knowledge with ease. Reinforcement is key to making crucial information stick.

How to Strengthen Memory:

- **Spaced Repetition –** Your brain remembers what it revisits. Go over critical information at regular intervals. If you don't, it fades—along with your ability to recall key strategies in the heat of the moment.
- **Visualization –** Your brain processes visuals faster than words. Attach images to key ideas to strengthen recall. The best leaders don't just store knowledge—they create mental maps for quick retrieval.
- **Mnemonic Devices –** Acronyms, rhymes, and chunking make information easier to retain. If you're relying on sheer willpower to remember everything, you're making it harder than it needs to be.

Focus: Maximizing Attention and Reducing Overload

Focus isn't a luxury—it's the difference between those who execute with precision and those who get lost in the noise. In today's world, distractions are relentless. If you can't control your focus, you can't control your outcomes.

Your prefrontal cortex (PFC) is responsible for decision-making and attention. But when it's overloaded—by notifications, multitasking, and endless mental clutter—your ability to perform plummets.

How to Strengthen Focus:

- **Cognitive Load Management –** Multitasking is a lie. It fractures your attention and drains your effectiveness. Prioritize high-impact tasks. If you let urgency dictate your focus, you'll always be reactive instead of strategic.
- **Mindfulness Training –** Your mind needs training just like your body. Deep breathing, meditation, and intentional focus exercises help block out distractions. A leader who can stay present in chaos is a leader who wins.
- **Deep Work Blocks –** Protect your focus. Carve out uninterrupted time for high-level thinking. No emails, no messages—just you and the task. The best decisions don't come from rushed, scattered thinking. They come from deep, undistracted focus.

Decision-Making: Balancing Logic and Emotion

Every great leader must master decision-making. But here's the challenge—logic and emotion constantly battle for control. If emotions take over, you make impulsive, short-sighted choices. If you rely solely on logic, you risk missing critical human factors. Balance is key.

Your prefrontal cortex handles logic. Your limbic system controls emotions. Under pressure, the limbic system can hijack your reasoning—unless you train yourself to stay in control.

How to Improve Decision-Making:

- **Scenario Analysis –** Gut instinct is valuable, but not enough. Weigh multiple outcomes before deciding. The leaders who dominate their industries are the ones who think beyond the immediate moment.
- **Mindful Reflection –** Impulsive decisions lead to regret. Take a pause—breathe, reflect, and give your brain space to process. Quick thinking is good; reckless action is not.
- **Emotional Regulation –** Pressure will push your emotions to the edge. If you let them run wild, you'll make poor choices. Use cognitive reframing and breath control to keep a clear head, no matter the situation.

Practical Application: Integrating These Strategies into Daily Leadership

Knowledge alone won't elevate your abilities—consistent execution will. Build these routines into your day to strengthen your mental edge and stay locked in under pressure.

Memory Enhancement Routine:

Start the day by reviewing key goals using spaced repetition to reinforce what matters most. Before meetings or critical decisions, visualize success—mentally rehearsing key conversations and strategies enhances recall. At the end of the day, reflect on what you've learned, reinforcing important takeaways. Memory isn't just about storing information—it's about making it stick.

Focus Optimization Routine:

Begin by structuring your day using the Eisenhower Matrix (*more on this later*), ensuring urgent tasks don't overshadow truly important work. Protect 1–2 deep work sessions where you eliminate distractions and execute with full attention. Throughout the day, reset your mind with two-minute mindfulness breaks—small but powerful moments that prevent burnout and sharpen focus.

Decision-Making Improvement Routine:

Before making major decisions, engage in scenario analysis—consider multiple outcomes and implications before acting. Be aware of emotional triggers that could cloud your judgment and distort rational thinking. When under pressure, use box breathing (inhale for 4 seconds, hold for 4, exhale for 4, hold for 4) to regulate your emotions and maintain clarity. The best decisions aren't rushed—they're made with intention.

Achieving Peak Performance in Leadership

Exceptional leaders don't leave their mental edge to chance—they build it with intention. They master the method, not just the motion.

By strengthening your memory, focus, and decision-making, you gain the clarity, resilience, and sharpness required to lead at the highest level. These aren't just strategies—they're the foundation for thinking faster, executing better, and leading stronger.

Daily Actions to Sustain Peak Cognitive Performance

Breakthroughs aren't born from big moments—they're built in the small, daily choices you make. Long-term impact comes not from hustle, but from precision and repeatability. It's about doing the *right* things consistently.

The three habits in this section are designed to elevate mental clarity, reduce stress, and create the cognitive space you need for exceptional results. Backed by neuroscience and built for the demands of high-stakes environments, these practices sharpen focus and increase emotional regulation over time.

These are the disciplines that separate busy professionals from impactful leaders.

Mindfulness via Breath Work

Breath control is one of the fastest and most effective ways to regulate your nervous system. This is more than just a tool for staying calm—it's your built-in switch for mental clarity and composure under pressure.

How to do it:

- **For Calm:**
  Use the 4-7-8 Breathing Pattern
  → Inhale for 4 seconds, hold for 7, exhale slowly for 8. Repeat 3–5 times.

  Ideal before high-stakes meetings, difficult conversations, or when feeling overwhelmed.

- **For Focus:**
  Use the 3-2-10 Breathing Pattern
  → Inhale for 3 seconds, hold for 2, exhale for 10. Repeat 4–5 times.

  Best used right before deep work, strategic problem-solving, or creative planning sessions.

Why it works:
Breathwork activates the parasympathetic nervous system, reducing cortisol levels and calming the amygdala—the brain's fear and stress center. This primes your prefrontal cortex, the seat of executive function, decision-making, and focus.

Why it matters for leaders:
When pressure mounts, your ability to stay composed directly impacts your team's trust and stability. Breath work keeps you centered in the midst of chaos.

Quick Tip:
Set a recurring reminder before key meetings or deep work blocks. One minute of breath work can shift your entire state.

Focused Work Sessions

Distraction derails progress, precision, and presence. Without structure, your attention gets hijacked by shallow tasks. Deep work—the kind that moves the needle—requires intentional design.

How to do it:

- **Schedule 1–2 Deep Work Sessions Daily**
  Block time for undisturbed, high-priority work. No notifications. No multitasking.
- **Follow the 90-Minute Rule**
  Work in 90-minute focused bursts, followed by 10–15 minutes of recovery.
- **Eliminate Distractions**
  Close unnecessary tabs. Silence your phone. Set up a dedicated workspace where your mind knows it's time to focus.

Why it works:

The brain works in ultradian cycles—periods of high focus followed by fatigue. Structuring your day around these natural rhythms increases output while minimizing burnout. Deep work also strengthens neural pathways for attention and creativity.

Why it matters for leaders:

Strategic thinking doesn't happen in between emails. Focused sessions create the space to solve big problems and make smart decisions.

Quick Tip:

Use a time-blocking calendar. Defend your deep work like you would a critical boardroom meeting—it's where real progress happens.

Digital Detox Before Bed

The brain needs downtime to reset, process, and restore. Without it, your cognitive capabilities decline fast—and so does your ability to lead.

How to do it:

- **Power Down 60 Minutes Before Sleep**
  Shut off screens, especially phones and laptops. The blue light disrupts melatonin production, impacting sleep depth.
- **Establish a Wind-Down Routine**
  Replace screen time with calming practices—reading, journaling, stretching, or meditation.
- **Create Clear Boundaries with Tech**
  Keep devices out of the bedroom. Make it a space for rest, not reactivity.

Why it works:

Exposure to screens late at night suppresses melatonin, delaying REM sleep and reducing sleep quality. Poor sleep impairs working memory, mood, and decision-making. A consistent nighttime routine signals your brain that it's time to transition into recovery mode.

Why it matters for leaders:

Rested minds make better decisions. Leaders who sleep well respond with more patience, better judgment, and stronger resilience.

Quick Tip:

Set an alarm labeled "Digital Sunset." When it goes off, shut it down. Treat this hour as the foundation for tomorrow's performance.

Lead Your Brain Before You Lead Others

These aren't flashy hacks. They're proven systems that sharpen your mind, protect your energy, and build a leadership edge that compounds over time.

Key Habits Recap:

- **Mindful Breathing:** Use breathwork to shift from stress to clarity on demand.
- **Focused Work:** Build your day around deep work to protect your brain's best hours.
- **Digital Detox:** End each day with recovery rituals that prime your brain for tomorrow.

Fast-Track Hack:

Choose one habit to start this week. Schedule it. Practice it daily. In 30 days, layer in another. Excellence isn't about doing more—it's about building better defaults.

The Eisenhower Matrix: Prioritizing What Truly Matters

The Eisenhower Matrix is a time management and decision-making framework inspired by Dwight D. Eisenhower, the 34th President of the United States and a five-star general during World War II. Eisenhower was known for his ability to distinguish between what was truly important and what was merely urgent, a skill essential in high-stakes environments. His approach was later formalized into this powerful productivity tool.

The Four Quadrants of the Eisenhower Matrix

The Eisenhower Matrix divides tasks into four quadrants based on urgency and importance:

1. **Urgent & Important (Do Now)** – Tasks that require immediate attention and have significant consequences if delayed.
2. **Important but Not Urgent (Plan & Schedule)** – Strategic work that contributes to long-term goals but doesn't demand immediate action.
3. **Urgent but Not Important (Delegate)** – Tasks that feel pressing but don't require your direct involvement—delegate these whenever possible.

4. **Neither Urgent nor Important (Eliminate) –** Low-value activities that drain time and energy—cut them out.

Here's a simple visual representation of the Eisenhower Matrix:

	Urgent	Not Urgent
Important	**DO NOW**	**PLAN & SCHEDULE**
Not Important	**DELEGATE**	**ELIMINATE**

How to Use the Eisenhower Matrix

1. **List Your Tasks –** At the start of each day, write down everything you need to accomplish.
2. **Categorize Each Task –** Place each task in one of the four quadrants based on urgency and importance.
3. **Act Accordingly –**
   - **Do** urgent and important tasks immediately.
   - **Plan** important but not urgent tasks by scheduling them in advance.
   - **Delegate** urgent but less important tasks to someone else.
   - **Eliminate** tasks that add no real value.

By consistently using the Eisenhower Matrix, you'll gain clarity, reduce stress, and ensure your time is spent on what truly drives results—not just reacting to whatever demands your attention.

From Burnout to Breakthrough: A Leadership Reset

My client Jeff had always been a high achiever. As a corporate attorney navigating complex deals and negotiations, he had built a reputation for sharp thinking, relentless work ethic, and the ability to handle high-pressure situations. He thrived on long hours, intricate problem-solving, and pushing through exhaustion to get the job done.

But lately, something had shifted.

The constant demands—endless meetings, urgent client calls, and the pressure to stay ahead—were taking a toll. Where he once felt sharp and in control, he now felt mentally foggy and drained. Decision fatigue crept in, making even routine tasks feel overwhelming. The clarity that had once set him apart was slipping, and with it, his confidence in his own abilities.

It all came to a head during a major deal negotiation. Jeff had spent weeks preparing, analyzing every angle, ensuring his firm's position was airtight. But as the negotiation unfolded, he found himself struggling to articulate his points with his usual precision.

His thinking felt slow; his focus scattered.

Afterward, we had a conversation that became his wake-up call. "You're running yourself into the ground," I told him. "Your ability to perform at a high level isn't just about working harder—it's about how well you recover, manage energy, and create the mental space for strategic thinking."

That moment shifted Jeff's perspective. He realized that the same drive that had fueled his success was now working against him. If he wanted to continue excelling, he needed an original approach—one that didn't just rely on sheer willpower but leveraged strategy, clarity, and sustainability.

The Shift: Rebuilding Performance from the Inside Out

Instead of doubling down on his old habits—working later, pushing harder—Jeff started optimizing *how* he worked, not just *how much* he worked. Through our coaching, he made key shifts in three areas:

Restoring Mental Clarity with Structured Focus

One of the first strategies we introduced was deep work blocks—dedicated time for high-level thinking without distractions. Rather than reacting to emails and fires all day, Jeff began structuring his calendar to protect his best thinking time.

We also implemented mindfulness techniques to reset his cognitive load. Just 10 minutes of focused breathing in the morning helped him clear mental clutter and improve his ability to stay present in high-stakes conversations.

The biggest shift? Moving from reactive to proactive. By defining clear priorities and structuring his workload intentionally, he eliminated the constant mental drain that had been clouding his thinking.

Optimizing Energy for Long-Term Success

Jeff had been sacrificing sleep, workouts, and nutrition in favor of "more time" to work—only to find himself operating at a fraction of his capacity. Together, we rebuilt his energy management:

- **Sleep as a performance tool:** Creating a structured evening routine to improve sleep quality.
- **Smart movement:** Short, high-intensity workouts that fit his schedule and boosted his resilience.
- **Cognitive nutrition:** Eating for increased brain power, focusing on nutrient-dense foods that stabilized his energy and mental clarity.

Within weeks, he felt the difference—steadier energy, clearer thinking, and no more afternoon crashes.

Refining Execution: From Grinding to Strategic

One of Jeff's biggest realizations was that *his approach to work was contributing to his own burnout.* He had been holding too much on his plate, convinced that his involvement in every detail was necessary.

Through coaching, we worked on strategic delegation—empowering his team instead of trying to do everything himself. Meetings became shorter and more effective, and his firm started running more smoothly as a result.

By shifting from an *always* on execution mode to a strategic and focused approach, Jeff regained not only his time but also his impact.

The Breakthrough: Sustainable Success

Within months, Jeff's transition was undeniable. His decision-making was sharper, his efforts more effective, and his energy sustainable. He wasn't just surviving his workload—he was thriving in it.

His biggest insight? Peak performance isn't about working longer hours—it's about structuring your work, energy, and recovery intelligently.

As Jeff put it: *"Before working with you, I thought success meant outworking everyone. Now I understand that real leadership is about clarity, focus, and creating systems that allow me to perform at my best—not just for a sprint, but for the long game."*

Now that you've seen what's possible when performance is redesigned from the inside out, it's time to expand your edge. Because high performance without emotional clarity will always fall short. That's what we'll unlock next.

Clarity in the Chaos: Leading with EQ Under Pressure

Emotional Intelligence (EQ) isn't just about "being nice" or "staying calm." It's about developing the mental and emotional agility to handle whatever comes at you. And let's be real—leadership will test you.

People will challenge you. Situations will frustrate you. You'll face pressure, uncertainty, and decisions that could make or break your credibility. And in those moments, your emotional intelligence is either your greatest advantage or your biggest liability.

It isn't your strategy, technical skills, or even your vision that determines your long-term success as a decision-maker. It's how you respond under pressure. It's how you deal with setbacks, navigate conflict, and lead people—not just when things go smoothly, but when everything gets messy.

If you don't develop your EQ, here's what happens:

- You react instead of respond. Your emotions hijack your thoughts. You say or do things you regret.
- You lose trust. A single unchecked reaction can damage months (or years) of credibility.
- You burn out. Because without emotional resilience, leadership exhausts you.

Successful executives? They don't let their emotions control them. They use EQ to stay clear-headed, adaptable, and unshakable—no matter the challenge.

This is your edge. If you want to lead with clarity, strength, and resilience, you need to sharpen your EQ. Here's how.

Strengthen Self-Awareness: Understanding Your Emotional Triggers

If you don't understand your emotions, they'll control you. Unchecked frustration, insecurity, or ego can lead to poor decisions, strained relationships, and credibility damage. Self-awareness is about recognizing your patterns before they undermine your effectiveness.

Here's how to take control:

Identify Your Triggers. Pay attention to the situations that consistently set you off—whether it's criticism, slow progress, or a lack of control. Triggers are patterns, and once you spot them, you can start changing how you react. Keep a journal or use voice notes to track moments when you feel irritated, defensive, or anxious.

Use Emotional Check-Ins. Throughout the day, pause for 30 seconds and ask, *"What am I feeling right now, and why?"* This small habit prevents emotional autopilot. If you find yourself frustrated, dig deeper—are you actually frustrated, or are you feeling unheard, unappreciated, or overwhelmed? Name it to tame it.

Get Honest Feedback. Ask trusted colleagues, *"How do I show up under pressure?"* You might not love the answers, but awareness is power. If multiple people say you come off as intense, dismissive, or impatient, don't fight it—figure out why and refine your approach.

Master Emotional Regulation: Responding Instead of Reacting

Leadership will throw stress your way—tight deadlines, difficult personalities, unexpected setbacks. If you don't control your reactions, they'll control you. Snapping at a colleague, shutting down under pressure, or making reactive decisions can cost you respect and momentum.

Here's what to do instead:

Pause Before Reacting. When you feel a strong emotional response building, stop yourself. Take a slow breath and ask, *"Is my reaction going to help or hurt this situation?"* A 10-second delay can mean the difference between an impulsive mistake and a strategic move.

Train Your Nervous System. Stress is inevitable, but how you handle it is a choice. Use techniques like the 4-7-8 breathing method (inhale for 4 sec, hold for 7, exhale for 8) to reset your system on the spot. Cold showers, intense exercise, and meditation also train your body to stay composed under pressure.

Reframe Challenges. Don't waste energy on frustration. When something goes wrong, shift your mindset: *"What's the lesson here? How do I move forward?"* Instead of seeing obstacles as threats, see them as tests of your ability.

Develop Empathy: Understanding What's Not Being Said

Most of us listen to reply, not to understand. That's a problem. If you don't truly hear your team, you'll miss opportunities, misread conflicts, and lose trust. Empathy isn't just about kindness—it's about influence, connection, and making smarter decisions.

Here's how to develop it:

Practice Active Listening. In your next conversation, resist the urge to interrupt or formulate a response while the other person is talking. Instead, focus entirely on understanding their message. After they finish, summarize what they said before responding. This small shift will instantly make people feel heard and valued.

Ask Better Questions. Surface-level conversations don't reveal the full picture. When dealing with team members, clients, or peers, go deeper: *"What's really driving this reaction? What aren't they saying?"* People often communicate through tone, hesitation, and body language—pay attention to those, not just their words.

Read Emotional Undercurrents. That difficult employee? Might feel undervalued. That defensive colleague? They could be afraid of looking incompetent. When you recognize the emotion behind the action, you stop taking things personally and start responding with intelligence.

Build Stronger Social Skills: Communicating with Impact

Leadership isn't just about making decisions—it's about getting people to buy into them. If you can't communicate your vision, navigate tough conversations, or inspire action, you'll struggle to lead effectively.

Here's how to level up communication:

Master Reflective Listening. Before responding to someone, restate their key points in your own words: *"So what I'm hearing is..."* This shows that you understand their perspective and prevents miscommunication. It also forces people to clarify their own thinking.

Own Your Nonverbal Cues. Communication isn't just what you say—it's how you say it. Pay attention to your body language, facial expressions, and tone. If you're frustrated but trying to sound supportive, your team will notice the inconsistency. Align your verbal and nonverbal messages.

Navigate Conflict with Precision. Instead of reacting defensively, approach disagreements with a solution-first mindset: *"I see where you're coming from. How do we move forward?"* Conflict isn't about winning—it's about alignment.

Cultivate Resilience: Leading Under Pressure

We all get knocked down. The difference? Resilient leaders get back up—faster, smarter, and stronger. Resilience isn't about avoiding stress; it's about training yourself to handle it without breaking.

Here's how to build that grit:

Develop a Growth Mindset. When setbacks happen, shift your perspective: *"What's this teaching me? How can I see failures as steppingstones, not roadblocks?"*

Use Micro-Recoveries. Stress accumulates. Reset daily with short breaks, deep breathing, or quick walks to stay sharp. High-achievers don't just power through—they recover strategically.

Control the Controllables. Instead of wasting energy on things outside your control, ask: *"What can I take action on right now?"* Redirecting focus to what you *can* influence builds momentum.

Sharpen Adaptability: Thriving in Uncertainty

Change isn't just inevitable—it's constant. If you resist it, you'll stress yourself out and slow your growth. The best leaders don't cling to control; they train themselves to pivot.

Here's how to strengthen adaptability:

Stop Fighting Change. Instead of resisting, ask: *"How do I adjust? What's my next best move?"* The leaders who stay flexible stay ahead.

Stay Present. Overthinking the future fuels anxiety; dwelling on the past keeps you stuck. The best leaders stay focused on the now, making clear-headed decisions with the information they have.

Regularly Step Outside Your Comfort Zone. Growth happens in discomfort. Push yourself into new experiences, whether that's learning a new skill, handling difficult conversations, or stepping into unfamiliar roles.

Practice Self-Compassion: Leading Without Burnout

If you don't take care of yourself, you can't take care of your team. Life is demanding, and if you're constantly pushing without recharging, you'll burn out—and when you burn out, your ability to lead suffers.

Here's how to stay strong without running yourself into the ground:

Reframe Setbacks with Self-Kindness. Instead of beating yourself up over mistakes, ask: *"What did I learn? How do I improve?"* When we refuse to forgive ourselves, we get stuck.

Prioritize Recovery. High performers don't just work hard—they recover hard. Protect time for rest, exercise, and mental resets, so you can operate at your best.

Celebrate Progress. Don't just focus on what's next—acknowledge wins, no matter how small. Momentum fuels motivation.

EQ in Action: Daily Habits for High-Impact Leadership

Building emotional intelligence isn't about having a single "aha" moment or reading this book and calling it a day. It's about daily reps. It's about strengthening the mental and emotional muscles that allow you to lead with clarity—no matter what gets thrown at you.

And let's be real: Leading others will test your EQ every single day.

- A team member pushes back on your decision—do you listen or get defensive?
- A high-pressure situation unfolds—do you stay composed or let stress dictate your next move?
- You get tough feedback—do you absorb it and grow, or do you shut down?

Here's the hard truth: If you don't actively build your EQ, pressure will expose your weaknesses. And when that happens, you don't just struggle—you lose trust, credibility, and the ability to lead effectively.

But here's the good news: EQ is a skill. And like any skill, it gets stronger with daily practice.

These three actions will reinforce emotional intelligence every single day—so when the real tests come, you don't react. You lead.

Improve Emotional Regulation: Build Resilience in the Moment

Let's get one thing straight: reactive leaders lose trust. If you let frustration, stress, or ego take the wheel, you'll make short-sighted decisions, damage relationships, and erode your authority—fast. Those that stay composed under pressure? They train for it. Every. Single. Day.

Daily Practice:

Start the day with 3 minutes of deep breathing to set a calm baseline. Don't underestimate this—your nervous system is either primed for reactivity or resilience before you even start your first meeting. Controlled breathing shifts you into executive thinking mode instead of fight-or-flight.

Use the 5-second rule when tension rises. When something triggers you—before speaking, before reacting—pause and take a deep breath. Five seconds of control can prevent a career-damaging outburst or an unnecessary conflict. High-level leaders buy themselves time before responding.

End the day with a tactical review: *Where did I let emotions drive my decisions today? Where did I stay composed? What's my key lesson?* This is how you build emotional discipline. Without reflection, you don't improve.

Leadership Impact:

Mastering emotional regulation means you don't get rattled. You don't make impulsive decisions. You don't let frustration influence your presence. You gain clarity, control, and credibility. Your team will trust you under pressure because they see you don't crack when things get tough.

Your Move: Start with one deep breath before your next reaction today. You may notice how that one pause shifts everything—before anyone else even realizes why.

Develop Empathy: Build Deeper Connections with Your Team

Your team isn't following your title. They're following how you make them feel. Leaders who dismiss, interrupt, or bulldoze through conversations create resentment. Those who listen, understand, and adapt create loyalty. And loyalty fuels execution.

Daily Practice:

In every meeting, lock in. Make eye contact, put your phone away, and listen without interrupting. People can feel when you're distracted. If you want trust, be fully present. This small shift will immediately elevate how your team perceives you.

Before responding to criticism, pause and ask: *What's the real concern here? What's their perspective?* Leaders with low EQ get defensive. High-EQ leaders ask better questions. When someone pushes back, assume they see something you don't.

Check in with one team member daily—not about work, but about them. Ask, *"How's life outside of work?"* and actually listen. People remember the leaders who see them as human first.

Leadership Impact:

The best leaders build trust effortlessly because they understand people want to feel heard, valued, and respected. Do this consistently, and you'll see people work harder—not because they have to, but because they want to.

Your Move: In one conversation today, fully listen before speaking. You might be surprised what you hear when you're not filling the space.

Cultivate Adaptability: Strengthen Your Agility as a Leader

Most leaders don't fail because they lack skill. They fail because they can't handle change. They panic, resist, or double down on what's not working. But leadership is about adapting in real time. If you can't pivot, you'll break.

Daily Practice:

Set the right mindset every morning: Before the day starts, remind yourself: *"Something unexpected will happen today. How I handle it defines my leadership."* This reframes surprises as challenges to rise to, not problems to stress over.

Reframe obstacles in real time. Instead of, *"This is a problem,"* say, *"This is an opportunity to adapt."* High-EQ operators don't waste energy on resistance—they redirect it into solutions.

Track your adaptability. Keep a small journal (or use voice notes) where you record moments you had to pivot, problem-solve, or rethink your approach. Review weekly. This is how you train yourself to see adaptability as a strength, not a burden.

Leadership Impact:

The one who stays steady when others panic is the one people trust. When you show up as someone who embraces change instead of resisting it, your team follows suit. You become the leader who thrives under uncertainty—because you've trained for it.

Your Move: When something unexpected hits today—and it will—catch yourself before reacting. You'll often find that pause reveals your next move faster than you think.

The Edge EQ Gives You

I'll tell you this—every great leader I've worked with has mastered emotional intelligence. Not one of them became successful by ignoring how they show up emotionally. The best leaders own their presence, their reactions, and their relationships.

If you want to be that kind of leader—the kind who commands trust effortlessly, navigates pressure with composure, and leads teams that want to follow you—start here.

EQ isn't a nice-to-have. It's the difference between leading powerfully and struggling through.

The question is—are you willing to put in the work?

If the answer is yes, then you're already ahead of the game. Now, go do it.

Part III:

Peak Performance and Flow

High performance isn't a grind. It's a rhythm.

Elite leaders don't just work harder—they operate in states of optimized energy and focus. This section explores how to harness elevated states, strengthen your body-mind system through the High Performance Triad, and build daily habits that create momentum without burnout.

Elite Execution: Transforming a Team with the Power of Flow

My friend and client, Jake, prides himself on his ability to lead. As a former ball player turned AAA manager, he is no stranger to competition, pressure, and elevated expectations. His first season at the helm is a success—his team finishes strong, the front office is pleased, and he earns the respect of his players.

But Jake isn't satisfied with a good start. In baseball, just like in business, resting on past success is a surefire way to get left behind.

The game is evolving. Managing a winning team is about more than calling the right plays at the right moment. It's about creating an environment where players can reach their peak—physically, mentally, and cognitively. It's about setting a vision for sustained excellence, not just for the players but for himself and his coaching staff as well.

Jake knows that winning at the highest level means engineering a system where individuals thrive, balancing intense focus with structured recovery, rapid decision-making with deep reflection, and instinct with innovation.

A Shift in Strategy

Jake has always relied on his instincts, his experience as a player, and the time-honored traditions of baseball management. But he starts to see that gut feel alone isn't enough in today's game.

The best leaders—whether in sports or business—are those who combine intuition with data, experience with innovation.

So, he rethinks everything.

Physical and Cognitive Optimization

First, he focuses on player health, not just in the conventional sense of conditioning and strength training, but on a deeper level. He works with sports scientists and performance specialists to integrate advanced recovery strategies. He is exploring the use of wearable tech to monitor sleep patterns, heart rate variability, cognitive fatigue, and stress levels, aiming to incorporate these insights into his long-term coaching approach.

This is More than injury prevention—it's optimizing game-day readiness. His coaching staff no longer relies on outdated assumptions about effort and fatigue. Instead, they analyze real-time observations to make informed decisions:

- When is a player in the ideal cognitive state for peak decision-making at the plate?
- How can they structure practices to mimic high-pressure game scenarios while avoiding burnout?
- What mental recovery techniques can they implement to help players bounce back faster after setbacks?

Baseball is a game of flow—long stretches of routine punctuated by explosive moments of action. Managing that rhythm requires mental discipline, not just physical readiness.

So, Jake introduces mental triggers to help his players enter focused engagement more consistently:

- Pre-game visualization routines to simulate game-day pressure before stepping onto the field.

- Micro-recovery techniques like controlled breathing between pitches to reset focus instantly.
- Post-game mental decompression rituals to prevent stress from compounding over a long season.

Leading the Leaders

Jake also turns the spotlight on himself and his staff. If he wants his players to operate at their best, he and his coaches must lead by example.

That means mastering clarity of communication—ensuring every message is delivered with precision, whether in a team meeting, one-on-one coaching session, or dugout strategy huddle. He refines how he gives feedback, focusing on short, actionable insights that players can implement immediately.

But this isn't about communication—it's about adaptability.

Instead of sticking to rigid game plans, Jake encourages his staff to experiment with innovative approaches:

- How can they structure practice differently to simulate high-pressure situations?
- What techniques can help players recover mentally from failures faster?
- How can they use AI-powered analytics to identify subtle patterns in opponents' play?

These are leadership decisions—the same kind that executives in any industry face when adapting to rapid change.

The Flow of the Organization

One of the biggest breakthroughs comes when Jake starts applying these principles not just to individual players but to the entire organization.

A baseball season is a marathon, not a sprint. Managing energy across 150+ games is just as important as managing a single inning.

By tracking player recovery cycles and game-day readiness, Jake and his staff can orchestrate the rhythm of the season:

- Aligning player peak-performance windows for critical matchups.
- Adjusting training intensity based on real-time feedback, ensuring players aren't overworked.
- Optimizing travel schedules to maintain cognitive sharpness on the road.

Momentum is no longer about the winning streaks—it's about building and sustaining a winning culture over time.

The Evolution of a Leader

Jake's upgrade doesn't abandon what made him successful in the past—it builds upon it. Refines it. He still relies on his instincts, but now they are backed by data. He still believes in hard work, but now he understands the importance of strategic recovery. He still holds his players to high standards, but now he gives them the tools to meet those standards sustainably.

Most importantly, Jake realizes that being a great manager isn't about making the right calls during a game. It's about shaping a culture of excellence, where preparation, execution, and recovery are engineered into a seamless system.

This is modern leadership—not just in baseball, but in any field.

The best leaders aren't the ones who work the hardest in the traditional sense. They are the ones who work the smartest. The ones who value both human connection and data-driven insights. The ones who understand that true effectiveness isn't about grinding—it's about mastering the rhythm of success.

Because just like in baseball, the game of leadership never stops evolving.

You might not realize it yet, but the very same triggers that helped Jake engineer team-wide peak performance are available to you— starting now. As you turn the page, notice what you begin to feel, because what you're about to read may unlock the state of clarity and confidence you've been seeking.

The Flow Advantage: How Elite Leaders Unlock Peak Performance

Moments of true clarity and creative brilliance are rare—but they don't have to be accidental. These peak experiences have a name: flow. Often described as *"being in the zone,"* it is a mental state of complete focus, energized engagement, and high performance. When leaders tap into this state, time compresses, distractions disappear, and decisions are made with remarkable clarity and confidence. It's a serious performance advantage.

For today's leaders navigating volatility and constant decision fatigue, flow isn't just a psychological concept—it's a powerful mental state that can be understood, triggered, and sustained. It's where pressure meets mastery. And the best leaders know how to engineer this state not only for themselves, but across their teams.

The Neuroscience of Flow: Rewiring the Executive Mind

Flow is more than a feeling—it's a neurological cocktail that propels the brain into an optimal state. Understanding what's happening under the hood allows us to become more intentional about accessing it.

Here's what's really going on:

Dopamine Surge: In this state, the brain releases dopamine—the neurotransmitter responsible for motivation, pleasure, and reward anticipation. This boosts focus, accelerates learning, and makes work feel deeply engaging.

Norepinephrine & Endorphins: These moments activate norepinephrine (enhancing alertness) and endorphins (reducing pain and increasing well-being). The result? An energized calm where leaders can stay sharp under pressure without burning out.

Alpha–Theta Brainwave Balance: The brain shifts into alpha (relaxed alertness) and theta (deep creativity and intuition) waves, enabling access to innovative, strategic thinking. Leaders often connect dots they wouldn't see in a more rigid or analytical mode.

Transient Hypofrontality: Perhaps the most fascinating element is the temporary quieting of the prefrontal cortex—home of self-monitoring, inner doubt, and overanalysis. This "strategic silence" reduces hesitation, allowing instinctive precision and confident decision-making in high-stakes moments.

Flow as a Leadership Superpower

This isn't about average productivity—it's an exponential multiplier. Here's how operating in this state improves real-world results:

Enhanced Creativity

Being in the zone accelerates creative problem-solving by reducing inhibition and increasing neural efficiency. Ideas connect faster, and bold thinking feels more natural.

Example: A CEO deep in strategic planning enters the zone during a vision session. Instead of grinding through possibilities, insights come in waves—unexpected but precise. They're not just solving problems—they're reshaping the future.

Laser Focus and Clarity

Operating in the zone sharpens attention. Leaders can silence distractions and lock in on what matters—without white-knuckling their way through.

Example: During a make-or-break negotiation, an executive in the zone reads the room instinctively, adapts strategy in real time, and stays composed under pressure—closing the deal while others react emotionally.

Faster, Smarter Decisions

With the prefrontal cortex dialed down, overthinking and self-doubt take a backseat. In this state, decisions come faster and with deeper intuitive trust.

Example: A product manager confronted with a last-minute failure doesn't freeze. Instead, they access their flow state, drawing from deep experience and pattern recognition to resolve the issue with speed and clarity—turning crisis into opportunity.

Command Performance

Whether leading a team, delivering a keynote, or pitching to investors, this state amplifies presence, adaptability, and persuasion.

Example: During a high-stakes presentation, a speaker fully immersed in the moment reads subtle audience cues, adjusts tone and message on the fly, and delivers with authenticity. It's not rehearsed—it's embodied leadership in action.

Lead in Flow or Fall Behind

This isn't a luxury reserved for athletes or artists—it's a strategic asset for the modern C-suite, and entrepreneurs. Understanding how to access this state unlocks an elevated tier of capability. And once you learn to create the right internal and external conditions, it becomes a repeatable advantage—not just a rare peak moment.

In the sections ahead, we'll break down the triggers that set the stage—and the daily practices that make it easier to access flow under pressure.

Maximizing Performance: The Leader's Role in Team Flow

Flow isn't just a feel-good state—it's an advantage rooted in neuroscience. Your ability to generate this state across your team directly impacts creativity, execution speed, and long-term resilience. Most leaders make the mistake of focusing on time management or productivity hacks. But the real edge comes from understanding the science behind flow and building environments where it can thrive.

The Science Behind Flow States

This state emerges when there's a balance between challenge and skill. Too much challenge? Anxiety. Too little? Boredom. The brain releases a cocktail of neurochemicals—dopamine, norepinephrine, anandamide, serotonin, and endorphins—that optimize focus and suppress the inner critic.

It's not accidental. It's triggered by specific conditions:

Clear Goals: When team members know exactly what success looks like, cognitive load drops and attention sharpens. Many leaders skip this step, assuming people already know the target. That assumption creates ambiguity—the enemy of this high-performance state. Clarity is oxygen.

Immediate Feedback: Feedback closes the loop between action and result, reinforcing learning and progress in real time. Lengthy delays dull motivation. Fast feedback fuels momentum. Keep it real-time, specific, and actionable.

High Consequences: The stakes must feel real. Whether it's mission-critical delivery or peer recognition, the brain engages more deeply when it senses importance. When everything is low stakes, nothing matters. This state needs gravity.

Uninterrupted Concentration: Multitasking kills it. Sustained, distraction-free blocks of time are non-negotiable for peak output. Protect these windows like you would a boardroom pitch. Because they are that valuable.

A Sense of Control: Autonomy fuels ownership. When people have freedom over how they work, they're more likely to lock in. If you're overprescribing the "how," you're robbing them of the possibility to engage fully.

Deep Embodiment (for physical flow): For physical or embodied tasks, like athletics or high-stakes interactions, presence in the body accelerates entry. Breath, movement, posture—these matter. Train your team to own their physical state.

You must build work environments that reduce friction and elevate focus. You're not just managing tasks—you're managing states. Your team's performance ceiling rises or falls based on your ability to design for deep engagement.

Leadership Psychology and Resistance Patterns

Often, we resist setting up the conditions for peak performance because it feels like letting go of control. Delegating more, eliminating distractions, or giving your team greater autonomy can feel risky—especially if your self-worth is tied to being the smartest or busiest person in the room. That mindset blocks real progress.

You can't engineer a high-impact culture while operating from fear, ego, or scarcity. Unlocking this kind of deep focus and creativity requires trust—in your people and in the systems you build.

Common Resistance Patterns:

Over-structuring: You build rigid processes and excessive approvals, thinking structure equals stability. But what you're really doing is shielding yourself from uncertainty. High impact results require structure—but it must be elastic, not brittle.

Micromanaging: You tell yourself you're helping, but the message you send is: "I don't trust you." Autonomy evaporates, and so does the possibility of deep engagement. This isn't about letting go of standards—it's about letting go of control addiction.

Fear of irrelevance: You stay in the weeds to feel useful. But what your team really needs is for you to rise above and design a clear, empowering system. Stop proving your value through effort. Prove it through outcomes.

Rewarding urgency over impact: If your culture is all fire drills and adrenaline, you're hijacking your team's nervous systems. Meaningful work can't happen in chaos. Stop rewarding fast starts and start rewarding meaningful finishes.

Addiction to being needed: This one is personal. If your value is tied to being the hero, you'll resist building systems that run without you. But your real legacy comes from creating something sustainable—where your absence doesn't mean collapse.

These patterns are often unconscious. They're tied to your identity— "I'm valuable because I'm needed." But leadership at the next level flips that script. You're valuable because you create the conditions for others to perform at their best—without needing your constant presence.

Creating a Flow-Conducive Environment

Set up your space and systems like an athlete would. Your physical space, team rituals, and communication cadence should all point toward immersive presence and deep work.

Environment matters: Remove friction. Noise, clutter, visual distractions—they all drain attention. Invest in soundproofing, clean design, or focused work zones. Provide optional core focus hours where meetings are banned and flow is protected. Think: fewer notifications, more intentionality.

Clear goals: Define what "done" looks like. Ambiguity creates mental load, which burns both glucose and attention. Clarity isn't a luxury—it's fuel for performance. Make it visible. Tie individual work to team-level purpose.

Autonomy with accountability: Give people control over *how* they work but never compromise on the *what*. Autonomy without standards breeds chaos. Standards without autonomy breeds disengagement. Let go, but don't drift.

Real-time feedback: Prolonged delays kill motivation. Feedback loops should be fast, specific, and safe. Use daily standups, short check-ins, or simple dashboards—whatever keeps your team calm, calibrated and moving. Avoid sugarcoating. Lead with truth, not comfort.

Ritualized entry into deep work: Athletes have warmups. Actors have backstage routines. Your team needs cues that signal, "It's time to focus." Consider using music, lighting changes, or even a short breathing routine before sprints. Help them anchor peak performance in predictable rituals.

Psychological safety: Fear shuts down the prefrontal cortex. Flow needs trust. Model vulnerability. Celebrate learning. Never punish intelligent risk-taking. Your team needs to know they can stretch without punishment. You set that tone.

You are the architect. Build a system that rewards presence, not superficial actions. The more intentional your environment, the easier it is for your team to do work that matters—without burning out.

Key Flow Habits for High-Performance Leaders

You don't get into peak states by hoping for them. You build them—through deliberate habits that shape your attention, your environment, and your energy. These three practices are foundational for my clients, and they consistently drive breakthroughs in their leadership and output.

Calendar Worship & Surrender

Forget "time management." If you want to operate in the zone, you need time ownership. That means treating your calendar like a sacred contract. This habit is where discipline *unlocks* freedom. It's not about doing more—it's about making space for high-impact thinking and execution.

Here's how to do it:

1. **Strict start and stop times:** Boundaries create presence. No fuzzy endings. No drifting into work mode all night. Treat your workday like a mission: with a launch window and recovery protocol.

2. **Reduce total work hours by 15–20%:** Want more clarity? Try delivering the same results with tighter constraints. Compression forces prioritization. Most executives bleed 2–3 hours a day on noise disguised as necessity.

3. **Schedule deep work blocks:** Set aside 1–2 distraction-free sessions each day—no meetings, no Slack, no inbox. Just you and the task at hand. This discipline is what separates professionals from amateurs. Protect these blocks like critical infrastructure.

4. **Add active recovery:** Breathwork, walking, yoga, micro-meditations—intentionally insert short, energy-rebalancing resets. This isn't slacking. It's system maintenance.

5. **Batch communication:** Choose one or two windows to handle messages. You don't need to be constantly "available"—you need to be strategically present. And not every conversation belongs in email. Real-time clarity beats asynchronous ambiguity.

6. **Design around energy peaks:** Know when you're sharpest—early morning, midday, or late afternoon—and anchor your most demanding tasks there. These windows aren't about time—they're about energetic alignment.

Challenge: Audit your week. Where are your focus blocks? Where are you bleeding momentum? Redesign your schedule like your future depends on it—because it does.

Active Recovery Days

You're not a robot. And if you're leading at an elevated level, your nervous system takes hits—constant decision-making, emotional labor, and problem-solving eat bandwidth. Active recovery isn't indulgent—it's essential.

What this looks like:

Cold exposure (ice baths, cryotherapy): Triggers a neuro-chemical cascade that boosts mood, reduces inflammation, and improves resilience. It's a physical reset—and a mental one.

Heat exposure (saunas, steam rooms): Promotes parasympathetic activation, detoxification, and recovery. Bonus: Great place for reflective thinking or low-stakes reading.

Nature immersion (hiking, long walks, forest time): Reduces cognitive fatigue, restores focus, and opens the door to natural elevated states. Walk until the noise in your head settles down.

Massage and bodywork: Reconnect with your body. This resets the tension you didn't even know you were carrying.

Pro tip: Keep your heart rate under 120 BPM. That's the sweet spot for active recovery—not a workout, but not total rest. These activities help your body recover and your mind reset.

Challenge: Build yourself a 1-day recovery experience—your own personal "off-site." Stack three recovery practices and unplug from digital distractions. You'll come back sharper than a full week off.

Daily Power Down Ritual

End your workday with intention—not exhaustion. This ritual isn't about logging off; it's about resetting your mind, clearing the decks, and priming tomorrow for momentum.

The Power Down Ritual:

1. Pick your Top 3 for tomorrow: Choose three needle-moving tasks. Not maintenance. Not busy work. Ask: *If these three got done, would the day count as a win?*

2. Block time for each one: Don't let tasks float in the ether. Assign them specific time slots. Boundaries create clarity. These blocks are non-negotiable.

3. Define "done": What does complete look like? Nail it down. Vague targets create vague effort. Precision drives traction.

4. Clear your head: Wrap up loose ends—send final updates, fire off quick replies, capture open loops. Then do a brain dump. Offload everything onto a list. Use the Eisenhower Matrix to triage.

5. Audit your habits: Did you honor your calendar? Compress work hours? Execute your shutdown? Track it daily. Keep the ritual honest and repeatable.

This isn't just an ending—it's a launchpad. Tomorrow's clarity starts with today's closure.

Lock In Your Baseline

You don't need 20 hacks. You need a handful of high-impact habits, executed with consistency.

1. Calendar Surrender
2. Strategic Recovery
3. Power-Down Precision

These routines are your foundation—the environmental scaffolding where deep work and leadership thrive. When they become automatic, you stop chasing productivity and start living in your zone of excellence.

Together, they form your **Xecutive Operating System— X2OS™:** the internal architecture that drives clarity, presence, and sustainable output at the executive level.

This isn't just about mornings or checklists. It's your embedded system for showing up sharp, grounded, and results-focused—no matter what the day throws at you.

Next up: A tool to help you track, tune, and automate these habits—because what gets measured, improves.

X2OS™ Tracker: Optimize Your Xecutive Operating System

Build your personal and team flow system—one habit at a time.
You don't manage what you don't measure.

This tool gives you a clear, no-BS framework to track, reflect, and refine the high-leverage habits we've covered. It's not about micromanaging your life—it's about installing a feedback loop that keeps you aligned and moving.

Use it daily. Weekly. Whatever rhythm fits. Just don't skip it. This is how you build momentum through clarity—not through grinding, guessing, or hoping.

Daily Flow Habit Reflection (End-of-Day)

Habit	Completed? (✓/✗)	Notes (What helped or got in the way?)
Calendar Surrender (strict start/stop honored?)		
Deep Work Block(s) Completed		
Micro Active Recovery Completed (walk, breathwork, etc.)		
Inbox Batch Processing (1–2x/day only)		
Energy Peaks Honored (was deep work aligned?)		
Power Down Ritual Completed		

Fast-Track Check-In: What was the *one* habit that fell apart today? Why? What's the belief or friction point behind that?

Weekly Optimization Audit: Block 30 minutes every week—preferably Friday afternoon or Sunday evening.

Wins:

- What worked?
- When did you feel most focused, present, or in the zone?

Disruptions: What broke your rhythm?

- ☐ Poor time boundaries
- ☐ Overloaded schedule
- ☐ Reactivity (inbox, meetings)
- ☐ Missed recovery time
- ☐ Mindset trap (e.g., "I need to be the one to fix everything")

Patterns:

- What's the consistent problem?
- What needs to change—behaviorally or mentally?

Adjustments for Next Week:

- What gets prioritized?
- What needs to be removed or compressed?
- Will I compress my work hours by 10–20% to increase focus and challenge?

Monthly Flow System Calibration

Every 30 days, zoom out. Identify trends and reset your system.

Score Your Habits (1–5 Scale):

Habit	Score (1–5)	Notes/Insights
Calendar Surrender		
Work Compression (shorter, tighter hours)		
Deep Work Execution		
Active Recovery Discipline		
Power Down Ritual Consistency		
Energy-Aligned Scheduling		

Flow State Frequency: How many days this month did you experience true flow?

Environment Check: Is your space helping or hurting flow?

- ☐ Too much visual noise or context-switching?
- ☐ Are deep work blocks protected?
- ☐ Are top 3 priorities getting calendar space daily?
- ☐ Is your team aligned with this flow model—or working against it?

Upgrade Commitment: What one habit, process, or boundary will you commit to upgrading this month?

Execution Tip

You can run this tool in a digital workspace (Notion, Roam, Evernote) or print and use it in a journal. Keep it visible. Ritualize it. High-level execution demands high-level awareness—and that means reviewing your process, not just your results.

X2OS™ Snapshot: The 3 Non-Negotiables of Daily Executive Performance

The Xecutive Operating System™ isn't a checklist—it's the rhythm that runs your day. These three non-negotiables are the core routines that keep exceptional leaders clear, composed, and effective under pressure:

1. **Calendar Surrender**

   Treat your calendar as a contract. What's blocked gets done. What's vague gets lost. Protect your time with the same intensity you protect revenue.

2. **Deep Work and Recovery Discipline**

   Carve out at least one focused, distraction-free block each day. This is where creative breakthroughs, strategic clarity, and high-leverage work happen. Follow each block with a purposeful recovery activity.

3. **Power Down Precision**

   End with intention. Reflect, capture key insights, and set tomorrow's priorities before the noise begins again.

Consistency in these three behaviors is the gateway to sustainable clarity and performance. You don't need a perfect system—you need a system that runs when life gets hard.

A Leader's Remaking Through Physical Health

One of my earliest coaching clients, Mark, had spent years building his Kung Fu dojo, dedicating his life to helping kids and adults develop self-discipline, confidence, and resilience through martial arts. His dojo was more than just a business—it was his mission. But over time, the stress of running the operation, managing students, and leading his instructors began to take its toll.

He prided himself on being a strong leader, but he started feeling drained, both physically and mentally. His energy was low, his workouts had become inconsistent due to nagging knee pain, and his stress levels were through the roof. Worse yet, he could feel his presence slipping. He wasn't leading with the same intensity and focus that had once defined him.

One evening, after a long day of classes, Mark sat in his office, exhausted. He watched his instructors finishing up, leading students through drills, and he realized something—he wasn't the leader he needed to be. He was pushing through each day on fumes, and it was affecting everything. His patience was shorter, his focus wavered, and his ability to inspire was fading. He knew something had to change.

Mark decided: He would take control of his health, just as he had always taught his students to take control of their minds. The first shift wasn't in his body, but in his mindset. He stopped making excuses and got clear on his goals. He overhauled his eating habits, eliminating the quick, processed meals that had been keeping him sluggish. He restructured his workouts, focusing on movements that strengthened his body without aggravating his knee. And most importantly, he found moments of stillness, practicing the same mindfulness he had long preached to his students.

The results came fast. Within weeks, his energy returned. His body felt stronger, and his mind was sharper than it had been in years. But the most profound change wasn't just in how he felt—it was in how he led. His newfound clarity and vitality spread throughout the dojo. His instructors fed off his renewed presence, and his students responded with deeper engagement. The energy of his dojo shifted.

One of his biggest markers of improvement was something he hadn't expected—a 20-point drop in his blood pressure. The stress that had been weighing him down was no longer controlling him.

"In just ten weeks working with Lex, I've gained clarity on my goals and a sense of calm, leading to improvements across my life," Mark reflected. "My blood pressure is down, and my staff is more effective—all because I'm more myself."

By taking care of himself first, Mark unlocked a new level of leadership. His journey proved that true strength isn't about technique or strategy—it's about showing up as the best version of yourself every single day.

The High Performance Triad: Exercise, Nutrition, and Sleep

Physical health plays a critical role in cognitive performance, influencing our ability to think clearly, make sound decisions, solve problems, and remain creative under pressure. The mind and body are deeply interconnected—what we do to nurture our bodies directly impacts how well we perform mentally and emotionally. By optimizing physical health through exercise, nutrition, and sleep, we can enhance brain function, reduce stress, and unlock greater creativity, all of which are essential for effective decision-making.

Exercise: Boosting Brain Function and Creativity

Exercise has a significant positive impact on cognitive function by improving blood flow to the brain, promoting the growth of new brain cells, and enhancing cognitive flexibility. When we engage in physical activity, our body releases a cocktail of beneficial chemicals, such as endorphins, dopamine, and serotonin, all of which help reduce stress and improve mood.

Neuroplasticity: Regular physical exercise encourages neuroplasticity, which is the brain's ability to form new neural connections. This supports better memory, learning, and problem-solving capabilities. As an executive, being able to think critically and adapt quickly is essential, and exercise helps maintain the brain's flexibility in those high-stakes moments.

Creativity: Physical exercise, particularly activities like aerobic workouts (e.g., running or cycling), has been shown to increase creativity. Exercise promotes the stream of oxygen and nutrients to the brain, enhancing cognitive functions like divergent thinking—the ability to generate many practical solutions to a problem. This can be crucial for leaders when seeking innovative solutions to complicated challenges.

Reduced Stress: Physical activity reduces cortisol levels, the hormone associated with stress. By lowering stress, exercise can help you maintain focus and mental clarity, even in high-pressure situations. As stress levels decrease, the brain can better focus on important tasks, improving decision-making and problem-solving.

Nutrition: Fueling the Brain for Optimal Performance

The brain is an energy-hungry organ, using up to 20% of the body's total energy supply. Proper nutrition ensures that the brain has the necessary fuel to function optimally. A balanced diet with a focus on healthy fats, proteins, and complex carbohydrates provides the essential nutrients the brain needs to operate at its best.

Healthy Fats: Omega-3 fatty acids found in fish, nuts, and seeds are critical for brain health. These fats support the structure of brain cells and promote communication between neurons. Studies have shown that people with higher levels of omega-3s tend to have better memory, focus, and overall cognitive performance.

Glucose for Energy: The brain runs on glucose, and it needs a steady supply to maintain focus and alertness. Eating complex carbohydrates (like whole grains and vegetables) ensures a slow and steady release of glucose into the bloodstream, providing sustained energy for the brain throughout the day. Avoiding sugar spikes helps maintain cognitive clarity and prevents energy crashes that can impair decision-making.

Antioxidants and Vitamins: Antioxidant-rich foods (such as berries, dark chocolate, and leafy greens) help protect the brain from oxidative stress and inflammation, which can impair cognitive function. Additionally, vitamins like B12, vitamin D, and magnesium are essential for maintaining mood stability and cognitive sharpness.

A well-nourished brain is better equipped to handle stress, make quick decisions, and stay focused during challenging moments.

Sleep: The Foundation of Mental Clarity and Decision-Making

Sleep is the most critical element in maintaining cognitive performance. It is during sleep that the brain consolidates memories, clears toxins, and restores its energy levels, ensuring that we wake up prepared to do our best. Lack of sleep, on the other hand, can severely impair cognitive function, emotional regulation, and decision-making abilities.

Memory and Learning: Sleep plays a key role in memory consolidation. During deep sleep, the brain processes added information, strengthens neural connections, and integrates learning from the day. For leaders, this means that proper sleep supports better recall of vital facts and a clearer understanding of issues, leading to better decision-making.

Focus and Attention: Adequate sleep helps regulate attention span and the ability to focus. Chronic sleep deprivation reduces the brain's ability to prioritize tasks, making it harder to filter out distractions and concentrate. In critical situations, where focus is essential, sleep ensures that you can tackle problems with a clear and undistracted mind.

Decision-Making: Studies have shown that sleep deprivation can lead to impaired judgment, slower reaction times, and a tendency to rely on intuition rather than reasoning. On the other hand, quality sleep enhances your ability to make fast, informed decisions by boosting cognitive abilities like analytical thinking, problem-solving, and strategic planning.

Emotional Regulation: Sleep is crucial for emotional balance. Leaders who sleep well are better at managing their emotions, staying calm under pressure, and maintaining resilience. Sleep helps reset the brain's emotional centers, reducing irritability and improving mood regulation. This emotional stability translates into more effective leadership and healthier relationships with teams.

The Synergy of Exercise, Nutrition, and Sleep

When exercise, nutrition, and sleep are properly aligned, the effects on cognitive performance are magnified exponentially. The physical health triad—exercise, proper nutrition, and quality sleep—works synergistically to promote brain health, reduce stress, and enhance your capabilities.

By prioritizing these three pillars of physical health, leaders not only improve their mental clarity and focus but also boost their creativity, resilience, and administrative capabilities. As stress is reduced and energy levels rise, you can approach demanding situations with greater confidence, creativity, and poise, leading to more successful outcomes.

For executives striving to lead effectively in high-stakes environments, embracing physical health as a cornerstone of leadership is no longer optional—it's essential.

Embedding the Triad: Strategies That Run on Autopilot

The secret to sustainable excellence isn't heroic effort—it's smart infrastructure.

Leaders are under constant pressure to make decisions, shift focus, manage conflict, and stay calm while driving results. That load demands energy, clarity, and resilience. You don't get there by forcing yourself to do more. You get there by making fewer things negotiable.

That's what these strategies are for: ingraining this triad—exercise, nutrition, and sleep—into your life in a way that sticks. When your baseline habits are aligned, elevated performance becomes the natural output, not an uphill climb.

Here are three foundational strategies to help you automate health as a leadership asset.

Anchor Habits to Existing Rhythms

We are creatures of routine. From morning coffee to evening shutdown, our days are filled with predictable micro-moments. By tying new health behaviors to these existing touchpoints, you eliminate the friction of decision-making and build consistency through association.

This strategy, known as habit stacking, leverages the brain's natural pattern recognition capabilities. Instead of trying to create time and space from scratch, you attach the behavior to something you're *already* doing.

How It Supports the Triad:

- **Exercise** becomes a non-negotiable when it's part of your morning start-up, post-lunch reset, or evening wind-down.
- **Nutrition** becomes more consistent when tied to existing decision points—calendar reviews, commute planning, even Slack breaks.
- **Sleep** becomes easier to protect when you stack wind-down habits onto the end of work routines, not into random times that depend on willpower.

Research Insight:

BJ Fogg's work at Stanford shows that behavior change sticks when it's attached to an already stable cue. This isn't about trying harder—it's about using your brain's wiring to your advantage.

Expanded Example:

Let's say you check your calendar first thing every morning. Anchor a glass of water and 60 seconds of movement to that ritual. No gear required. No "gym motivation" needed. Over time, this becomes an *identity loop*—you see yourself as someone who starts the day hydrated, alert, and active. That mindset drives more consistent choices throughout the day.

Engineer an Environment That Nudges You Toward Better Choices

Outstanding leaders aren't just disciplined—they're smart about what their environment allows and encourages. Your surroundings silently shape your behavior. They either invite alignment with your values or invite drift.

This strategy is about deliberate environmental design: removing friction from the behaviors you want more of and adding friction to the ones that pull you off-course.

How It Supports the Triad:

- **Exercise** becomes more accessible when your shoes are visible, your calendar has blocked time, and you've pre-committed to the activity.
- **Nutrition** improves when the default choices in your home, office, and travel setup support energy and mental clarity.
- **Sleep** becomes more reliable when your bedroom, tech usage, and evening rituals signal the body to slow down.

Research Insight:

This is the heart of choice architecture. Richard Thaler and Cass Sunstein's research shows that defaults dominate decision-making. When you don't have to think, you default to your environment's design. Those who understand this design with intention and win by default.

Expanded Example:

Your laptop shuts down at 8:30 PM. Your lights auto-dim. Blue-light blockers are on your nightstand. There's no TV in the bedroom. None of this is extreme. But it removes the friction around winding down. You're not forcing sleep—you're *inviting it*. Over time, your nervous system learns this is when we recover.

Run a Weekly Personal Operating Review

Every leader reviews dashboards—pipeline, product delivery, financial health. But very few review the only asset that makes all those possible: *their own physiology and performance readiness.*

This strategy is about setting up a weekly review cadence to audit your alignment with the Triad. It doesn't have to be detailed or data-heavy. What matters is consistent reflection, honest review, and small, real-time adjustments.

How It Supports the Triad:

- Exercise becomes strategic when you zoom out: Am I training for energy or depletion? Am I scheduling movement or skipping it during crunch weeks?
- Nutrition starts to work for you when you notice patterns—energy crashes, emotional eating, skipped meals. What needs to shift so your fuel supports your clarity, stamina, and decision-making?
- Sleep patterns emerge when you review data from wearables or subjective energy markers. Are you crashing midweek? Compensating with caffeine? That's a signal.

Research Insight:

Self-monitoring is a top predictor of long-term behavior change. According to the *American Journal of Preventive Medicine*, individuals who track behaviors—even briefly—are more likely to make sustainable health decisions. Forget perfection. Focus on awareness.

Expanded Example:

At the end of each week, take five minutes to reflect:

- Did I move consistently?
- Did I fuel with intent or reactively?
- Did I protect recovery time?

This simple practice builds a rhythm that mirrors how elite operators think—course correction *before* breakdown.

This Is a System, not a Hack

The strategies above aren't about adding more to your plate. They're about *designing your life* to serve your performance requirements. These aren't hacks. They're systems. And when those systems run in the background, your energy, clarity, and creativity move to the front.

Next, we'll break these strategies down into Three Daily Actions—simple habits that require no extra time or gear, and that you can implement starting today.

Mastering the High Performance Triad: 3 Essential Habits for Leaders

As we've explored, exercise, nutrition, and sleep aren't separate elements—they are interwoven pillars that support your ability to lead at the highest level. But strategy without execution is just talk. You need to embed these habits into your daily routine, consistently, so they become part of your DNA.

You don't need an hour of exercise, extensive meal planning, or eight hours of sleep to see results. What you need are small, targeted actions that prime you for a focused, high-impact day. If you take these three actions seriously, they will create a powerful feedback loop that builds momentum—and sharpens your edge. Let's dive into the specific daily habits that will make the most difference for you.

The 3-Minute Morning Activation: Exercise + Sleep Crossover

What it is:

The first 10 minutes of your day should be spent activating your body—not through caffeine, but through movement. A 3-minute sequence of light stretching, followed by a minute of bodyweight exercises like squats, lunges, or jumping jacks. The goal is to get the blood moving and the body awake. No equipment needed—just you and your focus.

Why it matters:

This early activation serves multiple purposes: it gets the body moving, primes your brain for the day, and helps synchronize your circadian rhythm, which is linked to better sleep that night. Think of it as the opening ritual of the day. Instead of diving straight into your email inbox or letting your body "wake up" passively, you're intentionally setting the tone for your body's energy and focus.

Research Insight:

Research has shown that early-morning exercise and exposure to natural light can help reset your body's circadian clock, improving sleep quality and mental alertness (Huberman Lab, 2021). This simple action not only primes you for the day but also helps ensure that you will sleep more soundly that night—critical for maintaining mental clarity and decision-making power.

Leadership Lens:

How you start your day matters. If your morning is chaotic, rushed, or lacks intention, you're setting yourself up for stress later. Leaders who move with purpose from the moment they wake up are the ones who make decisions with clarity and confidence. This is your chance to take command of your day—physically, mentally, and emotionally.

Quick Tip:

Aim to do this activation within 10 minutes of waking, even before you look at your phone or make your coffee. This is your power move to jumpstart the day.

The 1-1-1 Fuel Rule: Nutrition + Energy Regulation

What it is:

This action centers on fueling your body with the essentials it needs to operate at its best. Focus on these three key elements each day:

- **1 high-protein meal** (aim for at least 30g of protein)
- **1 color-rich plate** (vegetables and fruits for antioxidants)
- **1 hydration anchor** (at least 20 oz of water before 10 AM)

Why it matters:

Nutrition is the fuel for both your body and brain. You've heard the saying, "You are what you eat," but it's even more important to think about how you fuel your brain. Eating protein helps stabilize blood sugar, supporting focus and mental clarity. Hydrating early sets the stage endurance, and the antioxidant-rich meals protect your brain from stress and inflammation, keeping you sharp throughout the day.

Research Insight:

Studies show that high-protein meals improve cognitive function by maintaining steady glucose levels, while hydration supports both memory and decision-making (National Institutes of Health, 2020). A diet rich in fruits and vegetables also helps protect your brain from oxidative stress and supports mental clarity (Harvard School of Public Health, 2022).

Leadership Lens:

As a leader, you cannot afford to let your energy levels dip or your focus wander. You need to be at your best every single day. By prioritizing the basics—protein, hydration, and nutrient-dense foods—you are ensuring that your brain functions at peak capacity.

This isn't about dieting; it's about aligning your nutrition with how you show up.

Quick Tip:
Start the day by drinking a glass of water before even thinking about your first meeting. Follow it up with a breakfast rich in protein (like eggs or Greek yogurt). You're not just eating to survive—you're eating to lead.

The 8:30 Digital Wind-Down: Sleep Protection + Mental Recovery

What it is:
Shut down your work-related screens by 8:30 PM and spend the last 30 minutes of your day doing something non-stimulating. This could be reading fiction, journaling, light stretching, or walking—anything that helps you shift gears and prepare for a restful night's sleep.

Why it matters:
When we engage with screens late at night, the blue light emitted disrupts melatonin production, which can impair sleep. If you've been in work mode all evening, it can be difficult for your brain to transition into a restful state. This action helps ease you into sleep, allowing you to wake up feeling refreshed and ready to take on the day with a clear mind.

Research Insight:
Research has shown that even just 30 minutes of reduced screen time before bed significantly improves sleep quality, promoting deeper REM cycles (Sleep Health Journal, 2020). When you protect your evening with a digital wind-down, you're giving your body and mind the opportunity to truly recover and restore.

Leadership Lens:

Sleep is the foundation of every successful leader's performance. If you're not recovering properly, you're not leading at your best. This is about showing respect for your own well-being and prioritizing your ability to make strategic, thoughtful decisions. The digital wind-down ensures that you're setting yourself up for success in the morning, not just the day ahead.

Quick Tip:

Set an alarm on your phone for 8:30 PM to remind you to shut down screens. This is your non-negotiable commitment to yourself and your recovery. Keep your environment calm and quiet—no late-night email checking or brainstorming.

Your Edge Is Earned Daily

The beauty of these three daily actions is their simplicity. They don't require massive time investments, expensive supplements, or overloaded schedules. They are about making small, strategic changes that compound over time—changes that position you for success in both your personal well-being and your effectiveness.

Remember: This isn't about perfection—it's about consistency. By committing to these simple actions each day, you are building habits that support your potential and elevate your abilities, both mentally and physically.

As a leader, your most valuable asset is your ability to think clearly, make sound decisions, and inspire others to be at their best. These daily habits are the tools that will help you optimize your body and mind, and lead with clarity, resilience, and creativity. Commit to them now and watch your output reach new heights.

Part IV:

Resilience, Communication, and Creativity

*Lead through adversity. Influence with clarity.
Solve what others can't.*

Leadership today demands emotional resilience, bold communication, and creative problem solving. In this section, you'll learn how to stay grounded under pressure, amplify your presence, and unlock innovation through flow-infused design thinking strategies.

Resilient Leadership in the Face of Growing Pains

"Iron" John Gilliland, the owner of Stalwart Roofing, built his company from the ground up, quickly growing it to over $3 million in revenue. His success was fueled by relentless effort, strategic decision-making, and the same principles of leadership and performance that had driven him throughout his career. However, as with many fast-growing businesses, the rapid expansion outpaced his team's ability to keep up.

What was once an elite team began to struggle. Communication faltered, deadlines slipped, and the once-tight culture of accountability started to erode. Employees felt overwhelmed, processes became chaotic, and customer satisfaction took a hit. John knew that if he didn't act, his company's hard-earned success could unravel.

But John wasn't one to back down from a challenge. He recognized that the solution wasn't to work harder—it was to lead smarter. He needed to recalibrate, refocus, and rebuild his team from the ground up.

Rebuilding with Intent: A Fresh Start

John knew that patching the cracks wouldn't be enough—he needed to construct a stronger foundation from the start. Instead of trying to salvage a struggling team, he made the bold decision to rebuild from scratch, hiring the right people and instilling a culture of excellence from day one.

Hiring the Right Team: Quality Over Quantity

John isn't just filling positions—he is building a high-caliber team that aligns with his vision. Rather than rushing to hire, he is taking a deliberate, selective approach to ensure every new team member strengthens the company's foundation.

- **Character First:** Skills can be taught, but integrity, resilience, and work ethic are non-negotiable. John seeks individuals who take pride in their work, hold themselves accountable, and thrive under challenges.
- **Leaders at Every Level:** He doesn't just want employees—he wants problem-solvers and self-starters who take ownership of their roles and contribute to the bigger picture.
- **Adaptability & Team Fit:** Roofing is unpredictable, and so is business. John hires people who can think on their feet, adapt to changing conditions, and collaborate effectively under pressure.
- **A Shared Vision:** Every new hire must align with Stalwart Roofing's culture of resilience, quality, and teamwork. If they're just looking for a job, they're not the right fit—John is looking for people who want to build something great.

With this approach, John isn't just growing his team—he's curating a group of professionals who will drive Stalwart Roofing's future success.

Creating a Culture of Accountability and Transparency

Once the new team is in place, John will define clear expectations and build a structured environment where accountability is a core value.

He will implement weekly strategy meetings where team members can discuss challenges, align on priorities, and take ownership of their work. Every role will be clearly defined, and results based metrics will be introduced—not as a means of micro-management, but as tools for growth and success.

Mistakes won't be seen as failures—they will become opportunities to improve, refine processes, and build a stronger team.

Clarifying Goals and Streamlining Execution

John understands that a team without clear priorities is a team set up for failure. One of the biggest issues he faced before rebuilding was a lack of focus—too many projects running at once, leaving employees scattered and inefficient.

Now, he and his team will ruthlessly prioritize the company's efforts. Projects will be streamlined, distractions eliminated, and every initiative will directly support Stalwart Roofing's core mission and long-term vision.

To ensure execution stays on track, John will introduce a structured tracking system—not to bog people down with excessive reporting, but to create clarity, momentum, and a sense of progress.

Building a Team, Not Just a Business

A company is only as strong as the team behind it, and John will ensure that Stalwart Roofing becomes a place where employees feel valued, motivated, and aligned.

He will foster open communication, regular check-ins, and a culture of recognition. Wins—big or small—will be celebrated. Employees won't just be told what to do; they will be given the tools and autonomy to thrive.

Instead of dictating solutions, John will empower his managers and frontline workers to take ownership of their roles, make decisions, and drive results. The energy will shift—the team will be engaged, motivated, and ready to push forward with purpose.

Leading with Resilience

John knows that this isn't about fixing problems—it's about building a business that can withstand any storm. He will instill a mindset of resilience, adaptability, and continuous improvement.

Challenges won't be roadblocks; they will become stepping stones to something greater.

The Comeback in Progress

While Stalwart Roofing is still in the rebuilding phase, momentum will grow. Results will improve, processes will become more efficient, and the company culture will strengthen.

John's story will become a testament to the power of resilience. The comeback is still unfolding, but one thing is certain—Iron John isn't just rebuilding a company: he's forging a legacy of strength, adaptability, and unwavering determination.

The Lesson

Being resilient isn't about avoiding setbacks—it's about navigating through them with clarity, adaptability, and a focus on the long game. By implementing the right strategies, you will be able to steer your teams through turbulence and emerge stronger than ever.

Navigating Adversity with Strength, Adaptability, and Vision

Adversity is inevitable. It's also essential. It reveals the cracks in our thinking, exposes gaps in our systems, and tests the strength of our vision. But more than anything, adversity *reveals* us. It strips away the comfort of routine and demands something deeper—resilience, adaptability, and clarity of purpose.

History doesn't remember the leaders who coasted when things were easy. It remembers those who stood tall when everything around them fell apart. Think of Churchill during the Blitz, Lincoln in the throes of civil war, or Nelson Mandela leading South Africa out of apartheid *after* 27 years in prison. These are not just examples of calm under pressure—they are case studies in the groundbreaking change that adversity can produce when met with the right mindset.

As a leader, how you navigate adversity determines your trajectory—and that of the people who follow you. The tools you use, the habits you deploy, and the way you frame hard moments can either stunt your growth or accelerate your evolution. This section gives you a toolkit—tested, research-backed, and drawn from both neuroscience and real-world experience—to help you build resilience that lasts.

The Resilient Leader's Playbook: 6 Proven Strategies

Resilience isn't about bouncing back—it's about bouncing forward, stronger, and smarter. In high-stakes leadership, adversity is not a matter of *if*, but *when*. And when it hits, your response is determined by what you've built before the storm.

This isn't about feel-good quotes or generic grit. These are tactical, neuroscience-supported strategies designed to harden your mindset, sharpen your decision-making, and expand your capacity under pressure.

These six tools aren't theoretical—they're actionable. Each one gives you a lever to shift your mental, emotional, and physiological response to adversity. Master them, and you won't just survive the tough moments. You'll lead through them—with clarity, calm, and conviction.

Cognitive Reframing

Adversity doesn't just happen to us—it happens *through* us. Our perception of a challenge directly shapes our response to it. Cognitive reframing is the skill of consciously shifting your interpretation of an event. Instead of seeing a setback as evidence of failure, you learn to see it as feedback for growth. This mental shift is foundational to resilience.

In neuroscience, this process is linked to the prefrontal cortex—the region of the brain responsible for decision-making and rational thought. When you reframe a situation, you're engaging the brain's executive function to override the emotional reactivity of the amygdala. This is not about delusional optimism. It's about choosing a narrative that keeps you in motion rather than shutting you down.

For example, an executive who views a missed product deadline as a signal of team weakness will spiral into blame and micromanagement. One who reframes it as a data point about process inefficiencies will shift into problem-solving. The facts haven't changed—but the frame changes everything.

Stress Inoculation

Stress inoculation is the psychological equivalent of a vaccine. You expose yourself to manageable stressors in a controlled way so that when larger challenges arise, your system doesn't overreact. This technique, developed by clinical psychologist Donald Meichenbaum, helps build what researchers call "stress resilience."

You're not avoiding pressure—you're training your nervous system to handle it better.

Elite athletes and special operations units have used this for decades. You can apply the same principle. Running a team simulation before a major presentation, role-playing a high-stakes negotiation, or intentionally taking on difficult conversations weekly—these are forms of stress inoculation that reduce the fear response over time.

It works because repetition builds familiarity, and familiarity reduces threat. What once felt overwhelming becomes normal. You don't panic—you deliver.

Strategic Foresight

The most impactful visionaries don't just react to adversity—they anticipate it. Strategic foresight is the discipline of scanning the horizon and preparing for a range of plausible futures. It's what allows you to navigate uncertainty with confidence, not just optimism.

This is different from planning. Strategic foresight isn't about predicting the future—it's about rehearsing it. Scenario thinking, red teaming, and systems mapping are tools that train your brain to handle complexity before the crisis hits.

A tech executive who spends time mapping out how AI regulation could impact their product roadmap is not caught off guard when policies shift. They've already thought it through, weighed responses, and trained their team to think in possibilities, not certainties.

Foresight builds adaptability. And adaptability—more than intelligence, charisma, or even experience—is what separates those who crumble under pressure from those who rise.

Emotional Agility

Adversity doesn't just create external chaos—it triggers internal turbulence. Emotional agility, a concept developed by psychologist Susan David, is the capacity to be with your emotions without being ruled by them. It's the ability to name what you're feeling, make space for it, and choose your response.

Many leaders are taught to suppress emotion or hide it behind a mask of stoicism. But suppression doesn't create strength—it creates rigidity. Agility, by contrast, gives you freedom. When you acknowledge your frustration, fear, or sadness without judgment, you regain access to your full cognitive function.

Research from Harvard shows that naming emotions reduces their physiological intensity. This "name it to tame it" approach allows you to stay grounded in the storm. Emotional agility is not about reacting less—it's about responding more skillfully.

Controlled Exposure

The nervous system is a muscle, and adversity is its gym. Controlled exposure means intentionally stepping into discomfort in a deliberate, measured way—so that when real adversity hits, you've already built the internal capacity to face it.

This is different from stress inoculation in that it isn't about rehearsing stressful situations; it's about experiencing stress at a manageable level regularly, over time, to strengthen your ability to endure larger challenges. It's the principle behind cold exposure therapy or progressively more challenging physical feats, where each new level of discomfort teaches your body and mind that it's capable of withstanding greater levels of stress without breaking down.

For you, this could look like deliberately taking on more difficult projects, saying yes to uncomfortable conversations, or pushing yourself to present ideas to large groups even when the prospect of failure looms large. Over time, your resilience becomes a byproduct of repeated exposure to discomfort, and you become a more adaptable, powerful presence during true crises.

Stoic Preparation

Stoic philosophy offers one of the most powerful frameworks for facing adversity with calm and clarity. Central to Stoicism is the idea of premeditatio malorum—the practice of mentally rehearsing misfortune before it happens. By anticipating challenges and setbacks in advance, you equip yourself to meet them with poise when they arrive.

The goal isn't to expect failure or dwell in negativity—it's about preparing yourself for the inevitability of hardship. When you accept that setbacks will happen, they lose their power to derail you. This mental preparedness keeps you clear-headed and focused on the bigger picture, no matter the external chaos.

In practical terms, stoic preparation means having contingency plans, rehearsing worst-case scenarios, and grounding yourself in your values, so you can respond to challenges with wisdom rather than reacting emotionally. It allows you to stay rooted in what's important rather than getting lost in panic or frustration when adversity strikes.

Resilience isn't a trait you're born with—it's a capability you build.

These strategies are the foundation. But foundations mean nothing without daily execution.

Knowing how to reframe, prepare, or adapt is only the beginning—you need habits that embed those mindsets deep into your nervous system. That's where real progress takes root.

Because in the real world, leadership isn't tested in theory. It's tested in your calendar, your conversations, and your choices—every single day.

Up next: three daily actions that turn these strategies into your default operating system. Simple. Repeatable. Battle-tested.

Let's build the habits that make resilience automatic.

Mastering Adversity: Daily Actions for High-Impact Leaders

Adversity doesn't just test leaders—it shapes them. And the reality is we don't rise to the occasion; we fall to the level of our training. These daily and weekly practices are designed to sharpen your response to challenge before the pressure is on.

Think of them as mental and emotional strength training. When practiced consistently, they help you cultivate clarity under stress, emotional control, and the ability to lead through uncertainty. Each habit is grounded in neuroscience and 'practical first' principles.

Start with one. Make it a ritual. Then layer in the others. Resilience is built—not gifted.

Morning Adversity Mindset Priming

The way you begin your day sets the psychological frame for how you'll handle pressure. Morning priming isn't a motivational feel-good tactic—it's a strategic, science-backed exercise that conditions your nervous system for challenge.

How to do it:
1. Visualize one or two challenges you might face that day.
2. Mentally rehearse yourself responding with calm, creativity, and adaptability.

3. Add a quick journaling entry: one anticipated adversity + one strategic response.
4. Pair this with your morning coffee or five minutes of breathwork to lock it into your morning rhythm. Consistency, not duration, is the lever.

Why it works:
Mental rehearsal activates the brain's prefrontal cortex, strengthening executive control and problem-solving ability. This reduces emotional reactivity when real pressure hits. Studies on implementation intentions (Gollwitzer, 1999) show that when you mentally pre-plan your response to specific triggers, you increase your likelihood of success under stress.

Why it matters for leaders:
When your team sees you respond to pressure with composure and clarity, it sets the emotional tone for the entire organization.

Weekly Controlled Discomfort Practice

Resilience doesn't emerge in safety—it's forged under stress. Just like physical muscles grow through resistance, your mental and emotional strength expands when you voluntarily step into discomfort.

How to do it:
1. Once per week, schedule a controlled discomfort activity:
    - Physical: cold exposure, high-intensity training, fasting
    - Mental: difficult conversations, learning new skills, public speaking
2. Choose something that challenges your limits but doesn't overwhelm.
3. Schedule it on your calendar weekly. Treat it like a meeting with your future self—the one who leads better under fire.

Why it works:

This practice leverages the concept of stress inoculation (Meichenbaum, 1985), which shows that progressive exposure to stress in manageable doses builds adaptive capacity. Controlled discomfort trains the autonomic nervous system to regulate better under pressure—essential for peak decision-making and focus.

Why it matters for leaders:

Crisis moments are no longer novel—they're rehearsed. When real stakes show up, you already know how to stay steady.

Post-Challenge Review Ritual

Most people either avoid thinking about hard experiences or over-analyze them emotionally. Great leaders do neither. They reflect with intention, converting challenges into growth by asking the right questions.

How to do it:

1. After any high-stakes moment—presentation, conflict, crisis—set aside 10–15 minutes to reflect.
2. Ask yourself:
   - What went well?
   - Where did I struggle?
   - What could I do differently next time?
   - What did I learn about myself, my mindset, or my team?

1. Record your insights in a journal, a voice note, or a team doc.
2. Pair this ritual with your Friday review or debrief it with a mentor. The goal isn't to rehash the stress—it's to distill the gold.

Why it works:

Research on self-reflective learning (Di Stefano et al., 2014) shows that intentional reflection improves future performance by up to 23%. The act of writing or speaking your thoughts helps the brain consolidate lessons and shift from rumination to learning.

Why it matters for leaders:

Growth from adversity isn't automatic—it's a choice. When you pause to reflect, you compound your leadership intelligence over time.

Turn Pressure into Power

Formidable leaders don't shy away from adversity—they rise through it. Every challenge becomes a crucible, sharpening their strength, adaptability, and vision. By mastering these qualities, you don't just survive tough times—you grow stronger because of them.

When you build a resilient mindset, you gain the freedom to lead with clarity, even in the face of uncertainty. And as you grow through adversity, you inspire others to do the same—creating a culture of resilience that transcends individual challenges and empowers teams to rise, together.

The Adversity Readiness Tracker

Train for pressure before it arrives.

Leadership isn't tested when things are easy—it's revealed when the stakes are high. And your ability to lead through adversity depends on how you train when things are calm.

This tool gives you a structured system to build resilience one action at a time. It's designed to help you prime your mindset, lean into discomfort intentionally, and reflect on how you responded—so that when the real pressure hits, you don't flinch.

Use it daily. Review it weekly. This isn't about being perfect. It's about showing up and building the capacity to lead—even when things get hard.

Daily Adversity Readiness Reflection (End-of-Day)

Habit	Completed? (✓/✗)	Notes (Mindset wins, friction points, or adjustments)
Morning Adversity Mindset Priming		
Controlled Discomfort Practice		
Post-Challenge Review (if applicable)		

Fast-Track Check-In

- What challenge or discomfort did I face today?
- How did I respond—and what does that tell me about my current capacity?
- What's one small adjustment I'll make tomorrow to level up?

Weekly Resilience Audit: Set aside 30 minutes each week—Friday after work or Sunday before the week kicks off. This is your recalibration session.

Leadership Wins

- Where did I respond to stress better than expected?
- What decision, action, or recovery moment reflected strength, adaptability, or vision?

Pressure Points

What knocked you off balance this week?

- ☐ Unexpected change
- ☐ Emotional trigger
- ☐ Decision fatigue
- ☐ Avoided discomfort
- ☐ Overcommitment
- ☐ Leadership insecurity
- ☐ Lack of clarity or vision

What was the story you told yourself in that moment?

What could you have told yourself instead?

Patterns + Practice

- Where am I consistently avoiding adversity (or overreacting to it)?
- Which habit needs more reps next week—priming, discomfort, or review?

Adjustments for the Week Ahead

- What challenge or discomfort will I *intentionally* lean into this week?
- How will I recover and review after facing it?

Monthly Resilience Calibration: Every 30 days, zoom out. Measure mindset. Lock in progress. Reset where needed.

Score Your Adversity Habits (1–5 Scale)

Habit	Score (1–5)	Notes/Insights
Morning Mindset Priming		
Controlled Discomfort Practice		
Post-Challenge Reflection		

Leadership Capacity Check

- What type of challenge consistently elevates me?
- What type of challenge consistently derails me?
- What does that reveal about my current edges as a leader?

Environment + Influence Audit

- Am I surrounded by people who encourage resilience—or feed reactivity?
- Is my calendar built to support challenge and recovery—or constant fire drills?
- Do I model strength, adaptability, and vision—or just talk about them?

Upgrade Commitment

- What one habit, boundary, or belief will I reinforce or replace this month?

Execution Tip

Use this in Notion, Evernote, or your journal. Pin it where you can see it. Review it with a coach, a team member, or solo. Leaders don't rise in the moment—they rise from consistent prep. Resilience is built, not bestowed.

Command Presence: Communication for Executives

Success in today's business landscape hinges not just on knowledge or technical skill, but on influence, clarity, and connection. You can have the strongest vision, the most well-reasoned strategy, and breakthrough ideas—but without powerful communication, none of it moves.

That's the real battlefield for today's executives: a fast-moving world of competing agendas, short attention spans, and low trust. In that environment, your ability to cut through the noise and land a message that moves people should be your most leveraged skill. Every interaction—spoken or unspoken—either strengthens or weakens your influence.

The most effective leaders aren't always the smartest in the room—they're the clearest. They make others feel seen and heard. They speak with conviction, listen with intention, and create space for others to contribute. That combination creates followership and drives execution.

This section isn't about charisma. It's about repeatable strategies. These seven core communication skills are what separate average managers from executive-caliber communicators who own the room—and move results.

Clear Messaging: Cut Through the Noise

Clarity isn't a soft skill—it's a competitive advantage. When your message is clear, action becomes easy. When it's muddy, even the best ideas stall. Executive-level communication requires stripping out the unnecessary and drilling down to the core.

In a noisy, distracted world, clarity earns attention. And attention is the gateway to influence.

How to Lead with Clear Messaging:

- Start with the point. Don't build up to it—lead with it. Executives and teams alike tune out when messages meander.
- Use simple, powerful language. Ditch the jargon. Speak like you would to a sharp 14-year-old. Simplicity signals mastery.
- Reinforce your message. People forget 90% of what they hear. Repetition is not redundancy—it's reinforcement.

Active Listening: Lead with Curiosity, Not Control

Many leaders think they're listening when they're really just preparing their next response. True listening is a discipline—one that builds trust, sharpens your insight, and uncovers what's really at play beneath the surface.

When people feel heard, they feel respected. And that drives commitment.

How to Lead with Listening:

- Eliminate distractions. Put away devices. Give your full attention—visibly and audibly.

- Reflect what you hear. Say, "What I'm hearing is..." or "Let me make sure I've got this right..." to confirm alignment.
- Ask deeper questions. Go beyond the surface answers. "What's behind that?" or "What outcome really matters here?"

Storytelling for Influence: Facts Tell, Stories Sell

Information alone doesn't move people—emotion does. The most memorable and influential leaders are skilled storytellers who bridge logic and emotion. They use narrative to bring ideas to life, making strategy personal and values tangible.

If you want others to act, give them something they can feel—not just understand.

How to Lead with Storytelling:
- Use real moments. Share experiences from your career, your team, or your clients. Authenticity builds connection.
- Structure with intention. Set the scene, introduce the tension or challenge, describe the shift, and land on the resolution.
- Connect to meaning. Tie the story to the broader purpose, mission, or learning. That's what makes it stick.

Nonverbal Intelligence: Align What You Say with How You Say It

People don't just listen to your words—they read your body, tone, and presence. Any disconnect between message and delivery creates doubt. Congruence is what builds trust.

Your physical presence either amplifies your message—or undermines it.

How to Lead with Nonverbal Clarity:

- Own the room before you speak. Stand tall. Project calm confidence through posture and stillness.
- Match your tone to your message. Deliver tough news with composure. Share wins with energy.
- Read the room. Monitor reactions and adjust in real time. Micro-expressions and body language will show you how it's landing.

Conflict Navigation: Face Tension with Strength and Precision

Most leaders avoid conflict. Exceptional ones navigate it directly and skillfully. Conflict—when handled well—isn't a threat to cohesion. It's a driver of clarity, innovation, and trust.

The elevated approach? Address issues early, lead with facts, and model calm, clean communication.

How to Lead Through Conflict:

- Focus on facts, not stories. Stay grounded in what was seen or heard—avoid assumptions about motive or intent.
- Keep the tone forward-facing. "Here's what happened. Here's what it caused. Here's where we go now."
- Create space for mutual ownership. Ask, "How do you see it?" or "What's your perspective?" to co-create solutions.

Strategic Silence: Say Less. Mean More.

Silence is one of the most underutilized communication tools available to us. While most rush to fill the gaps, those who master the pause create space for reflection, authority, and presence.

Silence creates impact—when used intentionally.

How to Lead with Silence:
- Pause after key points. Give your words time to land.
- Hold space after questions. The deeper the question, the longer the pause should be.
- Be selective with your words. Trim the excess. Say only what matters—then stop.

Creative Framing: Position Ideas to Stick

Information without a frame is noise. Framing is how you make ideas memorable and give people the context to act. This isn't spin—it's clarity, applied with intent.

The best leaders don't just share data. They shape how others interpret it.

How to Lead with Framing:
- Use analogy and metaphor. Say, "Think of it like..." to make abstract ideas concrete.
- Reframe perspectives. "What would this look like from the client's seat?" or "What happens if we don't act?"
- Contrast outcomes. Present two paths—what we gain vs. what we risk. This creates urgency and clarity.

More Than Words: The Discipline of Impact:

Elite communication isn't about style—it's about substance delivered with precision. These seven strategies aren't tricks. They're high-leverage tools used by world-class executives to build trust, spark action, and lead at scale.

**Start with one. Practice it relentlessly.
Then layer the next.**

The path to greater influence isn't louder communication—it's clearer, sharper, and more intentional presence. That's how you own the room.

Communication in Action: Daily Habits That Build Influence

World-class communication isn't a gift—it's a system. And like any high-impact system, it's trained in reps. These aren't time-consuming rituals. They're small, deliberate actions that—when practiced daily—shift how people hear you, how they respond, and how quickly they move.

These habits are drawn from behavioral science, coaching psychology, and leadership trenches. Think of them as the compound interest of executive presence.

Prime One Key Message Daily

Train yourself to communicate with clarity and intent.

Before any meaningful interaction—a team meeting, a feedback session, an email that matters—take 3 to 5 minutes to mentally prepare. The goal: create internal clarity so you can deliver external precision. The best communicators rarely "wing it." They prime the message first.

Implementation Steps:
1. Ask yourself: What is the one message they must walk away with?

2. Define your tone: Calm? Direct? Encouraging? Urgent? Choose and commit.
3. Identify the outcome: What do I want them to do, feel, or think as a result?
4. Say it aloud once, or record a voice note and listen back for clutter or drift.

Why it matters: Pre-framing activates your prefrontal cortex—the brain's executive function center—shifting you from reaction to intention. In high-pressure settings, this small practice makes the difference between noise and meaningful communication.

Fast-Track Hack: Keep a running "Message Clarity" notebook. One page per conversation. Review weekly for patterns in tone, themes, or missed cues.

Ask One High-Value Question

Drive depth, engagement, and insight by leading with curiosity.

In at least one meeting or conversation today, don't start by sharing your thoughts. Lead with a question designed to expand thinking or surface unseen variables. This flips the script from directing to unlocking—and increases your team's ownership.

Implementation Steps:
1. Use question stems like:
   - *"What's the real blocker here—not just the surface issue?"*
   - *"What outcome would be a win in your view?"*
   - *"If I weren't in this room, what would you recommend?"*
2. Deliver the question—and wait. Don't fill the silence. Let it do the work.
3. Listen for assumptions, values, or unspoken constraints in the response. Note them.

Why it matters: High-quality questions increase psychological safety and invite problem-solving. You're not giving up control—you're building team capacity. Done consistently, this habit raises the level of thinking around you.

Fast-Track Hack: Create a personal list of five go-to "stretch" questions. Keep it visible during meetings until it becomes second nature.

End with Alignment

Turn every interaction into action through shared clarity.

Most communication breakdowns don't happen at the start—they happen at the end. People assume alignment that isn't there. Instead of moving fast, teams spin in confusion. This habit fixes that. It's how leaders close the loop with precision.

Implementation Steps:
1. Close every key exchange—meeting, call, check-in—with a clear summary:
   - *"To lock this in—here's what we agreed on, and here's what's next."*
2. Then ask: *"Anything I missed or misunderstood?"*
3. Send a one-line confirmation if needed. It reinforces follow-through.

Why it matters: Research shows that even brief end-of-meeting misalignments can lead to hours of lost work. Clear closure builds execution speed, trust, and accountability.

Fast-Track Hack: Use a shared doc or team channel to track alignment statements. Review before future interactions to ensure consistency and context.

Start Small. Stay Consistent.

Each habit takes less than five minutes. But when done daily, they rewire how your team experiences you. They stop wondering what you mean. They stop second-guessing. They start showing up sharper, thinking faster, and acting with confidence. That's the compounding effect of communication mastery.

The Path to Elite Communication

Great leadership isn't about saying more—it's about saying what matters most, with clarity, precision, and purpose. Whether you're guiding a team, a company, or a mission, your ability to communicate determines your ability to lead.

We've covered the core elements—clear messaging, active listening, story-driven influence, and more. These aren't just techniques. They're high-leverage tools to help you lead with impact.

But tools alone don't change you—habits do.

Real transition happens through consistent, intentional action. Daily reps. Small shifts that compound. Rehearsing key messages. Asking better questions. Creating alignment before you walk away. These may seem simple, but done consistently, they build trust, sharpen presence, and expand influence.

The difference between good communicators and elite ones? Commitment. Elite communicators keep refining. They incorporate immediate feedback. They stay curious. They lead with clarity—and let silence do the heavy lifting when needed.

Progress, not perfection. That's the path.

Leadership isn't just about outcomes. It's about the people you bring with you—and communication is how you move them.

With the right habits and frameworks, you won't just be heard. You'll be remembered. And more importantly, you'll be followed.

So now that you've explored the tools to lead decisively, here's something even more powerful—your voice. Because once you embed these ideas into stories, you'll see how naturally your influence grows. Let's take a moment to unlock that next level of leadership.

Storytelling for Leaders: The Essentials

Storytelling is one of the most powerful tools in a leader's communication arsenal. It's how you inspire, connect, and influence. But let's face it—many people don't think of themselves as natural storytellers. We tend to think of storytelling as a creative skill reserved for writers, marketers, or entertainers. If you don't see yourself as a "creative" person, you might feel like storytelling isn't for you.

Every visionary has a story to tell. And while storytelling is undoubtedly a creative skill, it's also a learnable one. With the right tools and techniques, anyone can become an effective storyteller—no matter their background or self-perception. That's why we're adding this bonus section: to provide you with a simple framework for crafting stories that are clear, compelling, and impactful.

The ability to weave stories into your communication style doesn't require you to be a born storyteller. It simply requires practice and structure. With the right approach, you'll be able to communicate your vision, values, and lessons in ways that resonate deeply with your audience.

In this section, we'll break down a proven framework that will help you frame stories that support your leadership goals. It's designed to make storytelling accessible, straightforward, and most importantly—actionable. The goal is to give you the confidence to tell stories that elevate your message and make it stick.

Four Key Elements for Impact:

The Setup: What Was Happening?

Every story needs context. Start by establishing the situation or the challenge at hand. This sets the stage for why your audience should care. You don't need to dive into too much detail—just give enough for them to understand the stakes. The key here is relevance. Whether it's a team challenge, a personal obstacle, or a business decision, make sure it's something that your audience can relate to or understand.

Example: "We were facing a massive product launch, and just days before the deadline, a major bug was discovered in our system. The team was under pressure, and it felt like everything could fall apart."

The Conflict: What Went Wrong?

Every good story has a moment of tension or conflict. This is where the action happens. You're showing what went wrong, what the obstacles were, and what was at risk. This is the part that hooks your audience because it presents the problem that needs solving. It doesn't need to be dramatic, but it should be clear and relatable.

Example: "The bug affected a critical feature, and without a fix, we wouldn't be able to meet our customers' expectations. People were stressed, tempers flared, and the clock was ticking."

The Shift: What Did You Do?

The most powerful part of any story is the resolution. How did you act? What decisions did you make? This section highlights your strategy and your role in navigating the challenge. It's the moment that shows your skills in action and how you led the team through adversity. The "shift" could be a decision, a breakthrough idea, or a change in approach.

Example: "I called a team huddle, and instead of assigning blame, I framed the challenge as an opportunity. We focused on collaboration and took a step-by-step approach to isolate the bug, divide tasks, and test possible solutions."

The Outcome: What Changed?

Finally, show the results. What happened because of your actions? This is where you reinforce the "why" behind the story. Did the team achieve success? Did the company learn something valuable? The outcome needs to tie back to the lesson or insight that is relevant to your audience.

Example: "Thanks to the team's hard work and our collaborative effort, we fixed the issue and launched on time. But more importantly, we grew stronger as a team. We learned the value of clear communication under pressure, and that trust is the foundation of overcoming obstacles together."

Storytelling Tool: The 3-2-1 Method

This is a condensed version of the framework above that you can use when you're short on time but need to deliver a quick, impactful story.

- 3 – What were **3 key facts** or pieces of context that set the scene?
- 2 – What were **2 key obstacles** you had to overcome?
- 1 – What was the **1 key action** you took to resolve the situation?
- 1 – What was the **1 outcome** that followed from your action?

This method helps you simplify and focus your story for quick impact without losing the key elements that make it compelling.

How to Use This Framework

Practice: Start by applying this framework in low-risk settings. Share a story at the beginning of a meeting, with a colleague, or even at home. The more you practice, the easier it becomes to do it on the fly.

Tailor It: Depending on your audience, tweak the details. A story for the C-suite will differ from one shared with front-line employees, or clients. Make sure your story resonates with the values or challenges of the group you're speaking to.

Tell Real Stories: Authenticity is key. People connect with real stories that show vulnerability and growth, not just triumphs. Don't be afraid to share moments of struggle or lessons learned.

Command Attention. Lead with Stories. Drive Action.

Mastering storytelling isn't about entertaining—it's about connecting. By using this framework, you'll not only make your stories easier to deliver but also more meaningful. When you tell stories well, you create emotional connections that inspire action, build trust, and drive alignment with your vision. Stories have the power to make your message unforgettable, giving your audience a clear, compelling reason to follow you.

GYM

Reinventing Back Bay Fit: From Hustle to High-Performance Growth

Johnny, the hands-on founder of Back Bay Fit, had built his gym into a respected name in the local fitness industry. Known for its personalized training and high-touch client experience, Back Bay Fit had long thrived on Johnny's relentless work ethic. But as online fitness influencers, AI-driven coaching, and low-cost digital platforms flooded the market, he faced a harsh reality: Growth had stalled. Competing on volume wasn't sustainable.

For years, Johnny had operated with a mindset of maximum revenue generation, believing that more clients, more hours, and more hustle were the only ways to grow. But as he looked ahead, he realized that he needed a fundamental shift—not just in strategy, but in how he approached work, and life.

Reevaluating the Business Model

Instead of reacting to the market, Johnny took a step back and identified the key business priorities that truly mattered. He asked himself:

- What services moved the needle for clients and the business?
- Where was time and energy being wasted?
- How could Back Bay Fit differentiate itself in an industry obsessed with convenience and automation?

The answer wasn't chasing more—it was focusing on better. Johnny leaned into client feedback and realized that his most committed clients weren't looking for another generic fitness program. They wanted high-impact, personalized coaching that no online program could match.

He restructured Back Bay Fit around a premium, high-touch experience, offering:

- Exclusive, high-ticket coaching programs that included custom health markers, in-depth assessments, and one-on-one training.
- Data-driven planning and tracking tools to enhance client results.
- A realigned team approach, ensuring his on-site trainers were fully aligned with the new mission.

The Power of Focused Effort

To execute this shift, Johnny knew he had to change how he worked, not just what he worked on. He implemented focused flow blocks—dedicated, distraction-free time slots for:

- Creative problem-solving sessions to generate new ideas and innovative strategies.
- Strategic planning to align his team and ensure long-term growth.
- Deep work on client services, optimizing every touchpoint in the Back Bay Fit experience.

To create a sense of urgency and efficiency, Johnny set strict start and stop times for work, breaking free from the "always on" grind that had once consumed his life. This forced him to be more intentional and effective with his time—rather than letting his days be dictated by endless tasks and distractions.

The Results: A Smarter, More Profitable Business

One year later, the numbers told a powerful story:

- Revenue decreased by 12 percent, but...
- Hours worked dropped by 18 percent, allowing Johnny to spend more time with his wife and newborn daughter.
- Total expenditures decreased by 22 percent, thanks to a leaner, more efficient operation.
- Total profit increased by 57 percent, proving that focusing on premium services over volume led to greater financial success.

But beyond the numbers, the biggest win was freedom. Johnny no longer felt like he was running on a treadmill he couldn't step off. He had more time, more clarity, and more energy—not just for his business, but for his life.

The Lesson: Sometimes, Less Is More

Johnny didn't scale Back Bay Fit by working harder—he scaled it by working smarter.

He got ruthless about priorities. Protected his flow blocks like gold. Enforced boundaries most only talk about. The result? A shift from hustle and volume to clarity and impact. Back Bay Fit didn't just stabilize. It leveled up.

Johnny's no longer stuck in the grind—he's steering a business that's *thriving* because he chose to lead from flow, not fear.

Now imagine for a moment—what if the same clarity Johnny found could become your operating system for transformation? You don't need to force it. The next few pages are designed to unlock that clarity and help you lead with more purpose, power, and precision than ever before.

Unlocking Innovation: Creative Problem Solving with the Flow Design Matrix™

In a world increasingly driven by machines, one human skill rises above the rest: creative problem solving. This isn't merely a "nice to have"—it's an imperative.

According to the World Economic Forum, *creative problem solving* consistently ranks among the top five skills most valued by employers. Why? Because it can't be automated. It's messy. It's intuitive. It's emotional. It requires nuance, connection, and real-time judgment—things machines don't do well. And in leadership, it's the difference between reacting and reinventing.

Most of us don't create the conditions for great problem solving. We think harder instead of thinking differently. They chase efficiency instead of insight. And they spend most of their day context-switching, multitasking, or reacting to noise—when breakthrough thinking demands deep focus and presence.

That's where Flow and Design Thinking come in.

When integrated intentionally, these two disciplines form the Flow Design Matrix™—a structured, high-performance model for creative problem solving. This matrix aligns each phase of Design Thinking with flow triggers that amplify creativity, accelerate insight, and sharpen clarity under pressure.

- **Design Thinking** gives you a structured method to approach pervasive, human-centered challenges—driven by empathy, iteration, and testing.
- **Flow** puts your brain in its peak creative state—highly focused, energized, and fully immersed in the task at hand.

Individually, they're powerful. Together, they're game-changing.

The Stanford d.school pioneered Design Thinking as a way to bring real-world innovation to life—starting with empathy, not execution. And for decades, researchers like Mihaly Csikszentmihalyi have mapped the psychological state of flow as the optimal zone for performance and creativity.

When you integrate them, you unlock a process that is both structured *and* fluid. Strategic *and* imaginative. This is how elite executives solve big, messy, high-stakes problems—faster and with more impact.

In the following section, we'll break down both strategies in depth, show how they combine, and give you simple daily actions to wire these habits into how you think, create, and lead.

Because in the future, the edge won't go to the most technical—it'll go to the most imaginative.

Strategies for Creative Problem Solving

Engineer Flow, Don't Chase It

Flow isn't luck—it's architecture. World-class leaders engineer it by mastering three variables:

- **Distraction:** Eliminate noise. Block your calendar. Silence notifications. Use noise-canceling tools and restructure your space to protect deep work hours.

- **Focus:** Build a ritual before every deep work session—breathe, stretch, set intention. Most of us think we're focused, but neuroscience says otherwise.
- **Challenge:** The sweet spot lies in the 4% zone—just beyond your current capability. Push yourself, but don't break. Break down big tasks into manageable wins, and if it's too easy, raise the stakes.

Pro Insight: Even a 2-minute mindfulness pause can improve focus and creative accuracy, according to *Nature Neuroscience* (2021).

Adopt a Design Thinking Mindset

Design Thinking, pioneered by Stanford's d.school and IDEO, isn't just a process—it's a mindset for solving human-centered problems.

At its core, it asks leaders to:

- **Empathize:** Understand problems through lived human experience.
- **Define:** Frame the real issue—not just the loudest one.
- **Ideate:** Generate many ideas before picking one. Creativity thrives on quantity.
- **Prototype:** Create quick, rough versions to accelerate learning.
- **Test:** Observe genuine reactions. Let reality shape iteration.

This mindset shifts you from *expert with answers to explorer of insight*. You stop assuming—and start discovering.

Now let's explore how executives fuse these two tools into a creative problem-solving superpower.

Introducing the Flow Design Matrix™: Integration for Breakthrough Results

As the speed of change accelerates and automation reshapes industries, the ability to adapt with creativity has become a defining trait of exceptional leaders. Creative problem solving isn't just about innovation—it's about adaptability.

It draws on distinctly human strengths: intuition, empathy, and the ability to connect seemingly unrelated dots. It's the skill that enables us to guide teams through uncertainty with clarity and conviction.

To master creative problem solving at the executive level, you need two things:

- A repeatable framework to structure your thinking,
- And a high-performance state to do your best thinking.

Together, these elements form the Flow Design Matrix™—a practical model that aligns each stage of Design Thinking with the triggers and leadership behaviors that drive creativity, clarity, and execution.

The Flow Design Matrix™

Design Thinking Phase	Flow Activation Strategy	Key Executive Behavior
Empathize	Deep presence and focused listening	Create immersive, distraction-free user sessions
Define	Focused framing with clarity goals	Craft one clear problem statement to unlock drive
Ideate	Uninhibited creative volume	Run fast, judgment-free ideation sessions
Prototype	Embodied experimentation	Build quickly with hands-on, tactile tools
Test	Real-time feedback integration	Use pattern recognition and emotional intelligence to refine solutions

Design Thinking gives you a proven structure for tackling complex, messy, human-centered problems. Flow activates your cognitive superpowers—deep focus, rapid learning, and creative insight—that make problem solving faster and smarter.

Combined, they give you a playbook for creative breakthroughs under pressure.

Inside the Flow Design Matrix™: Strategic Integration of Flow into Innovation

Design Thinking is a proven roadmap for innovation. Flow is the state that unlocks peak human potential. On their own, each is powerful. But when combined intentionally, they accelerate insight, collapse timelines, and make problems solvable in motion.

Flow isn't something you wait for. It's something you build into your daily rhythms. Here's how leading executives embed it into every phase of the Design Thinking process:

Empathize: Trigger Flow Through Deep Presence

Empathy isn't just about understanding others—it's about fully entering their world. That level of immersion requires more than listening; it demands total cognitive engagement. This is where optimal states begin. In these moments, when you're not solving but sensing, when you're not managing but deeply connecting, you create the exact neural conditions that allow heightened focus to ignite.

- **Schedule 60–90 minutes of uninterrupted time** for user interviews or team sessions.
- **Hold these during your cognitive peak** (usually mid-morning).
- **Use active listening tools** like mirroring, paraphrasing, and open-ended follow-ups.
- **Kill all distractions**—close laptops, silence devices, go analog if needed.

Define: Achieve Flow Through Focused Framing

You can't enter peak states when the problem is vague. Ambiguity stalls action. But when a challenge is clearly defined, your brain shifts into drive mode—locked in, focused, energized to close the gap between problem and possibility. This phase is about distillation, not detail. The more precise the framing, the easier it is to spark intense concentration in the team and move forward with confidence.

- **Time-box the framing session** to 20–30 minutes with a clear goal: one powerful problem statement.
- **Use collaborative tools** like whiteboards or shared docs to anchor focus.
- **Do a clarity pulse-check** at the end—everyone scores the alignment from 1–10.

Ideate: Unlock Flow with Uninhibited Creation

This is the playground of high-level engagement—fast, experimental, idea-rich. Great problem-solvers know that creativity isn't neat or logical at this stage; it's messy, nonlinear, and wild. Flow thrives here because you're leaning into novelty, risk, and ambiguity without the pressure to be "right." This is where real breakthroughs happen—not because you force them, but because you allow them.

- **Set playful constraints** like "sketch only," "no jargon," or "bad ideas first."
- **Aim for volume, not perfection**—target 30–50 ideas in 20 minutes.
- **Create psychological safety**—make it clear that this is a no-judgment zone.

Prototype: Build Flow Through Embodied Iteration

Flow amplifies when ideas become physical. Whether it's a sketch, a mockup, or a simulated process, bringing your concept into form invites deeper engagement. The body joins the brain. Momentum builds. Executives who prototype quickly don't just get answers faster—they enter a loop of tactile feedback and rapid refinement, which locks them into the present moment where productive engagement thrives.

- **Use hands-on tools**—paper, cardboard, whiteboards, roleplay exercises.
- **Keep the goal clear:** provoke insight, not perfection.
- **Work in short sprints** (30–60 minutes) to avoid over-polishing.

Test: Sustain Flow with Real-Time Feedback & Pattern Recognition

The testing phase is often the most underutilized—and yet, it's where flow shows up in unexpected ways. When you're fully present with users, tuned into their reactions, and adjusting in real time, you're engaging your pattern recognition and emotional intelligence at full tilt. This isn't just evaluation. It's performance. And flow rewards it with intuition, speed, and depth of insight.

- **Prime presence** with 5 minutes of silence or breathwork before test sessions.
- **Use curiosity-based prompts:** "What surprised you?" "Where did it feel off?"
- **Synthesize learnings fast**—dot voting, keyword clustering, or shared Google Jamboards.

Creative mastery isn't just built through insight—it's strengthened through practice, reflection, and the right environment.

Flow Design Matrix Toolkit: Daily Actions to Build Creative Capacity

The strategy gave you the map. These daily reps hardwire the mindset. Think of them as mental strength training for innovation: compact, focused, and high leverage. Use them to sharpen creativity, expand empathy, and make problem-solving a reflex—not a lucky break.

The Empathy Pulse Check

Build your insight muscle through consistent emotional awareness.

Every day, schedule 10 intentional minutes to step into someone else's experience—no fixing, just sensing. This could be a teammate, a customer, a stakeholder, or even your family. The goal is to uncover emotional friction—frustration, hesitation, confusion—before it shows up as resistance or churn.

Implementation Steps:

1. Ask one friction-seeking question: "What's harder than it should be right now?" or "Where are you stuck this week?"
2. Stay silent and present—don't jump in with solutions. Just observe.

3. Capture what you learn in a friction journal (physical or digital).
4. Review patterns weekly—top recurring themes become innovation fuel.

Why it matters: The best solutions come from problems you've felt, not just analyzed. Emotional friction often signals unmet needs others overlook.

Fast-Track Hack: Block 10 minutes on your calendar today—Empathy 10. You'll find this simple practice reshapes how you listen, without needing to force it.

Daily Flow Sprint: Define → Ideate → Prototype in 60 Minutes

Prime your brain and your team for creative output—on demand.

This is your daily discipline to stay sharp. Choose a real-world challenge (internal or customer-facing). Then run a self-contained creative cycle. By compressing time and adding playful constraints, you ignite the right triggers: clear goals, novelty, and immediate feedback.

Implementation Steps:

1. **Define (15 mins)** – Write a problem statement using "How might we..." or "What would it take to..."
2. **Ideate (20 mins)** – Generate 15–20 ideas. Push for edge cases, absurdity, or constraint-bending.
3. **Prototype (20 mins)** – Pick one idea. Sketch it, role-play it, storyboard it—don't perfect it, express it.

Why it works: This hits the Flow Cycle head-on: struggle →
release → flow. And it mirrors the brain's preferred rhythm of
creative production.

Fast-Track Hack: Add music, sketchpads, or a fresh environment to ignite divergent thinking. These subtle shifts often unlock
momentum before you even notice it.

Build Something Tangible—Every Single Day

Turn ideas into visible form to strengthen innovation throughput.

Prototyping isn't about perfect products—it's about directional
learning. The medium doesn't matter. The motion does. Executives
who train this daily become less precious about perfection and
more obsessed with learning speed.

Implementation Steps:

1. Pick one thing to prototype today—a new agenda format,
    customer script, deck concept, or dashboard view.
2. Give yourself 20 minutes max—fast enough to stay fluid,
    long enough to create signal.
3. Send it to someone you trust for quick feedback: "What's
    one thing this gets right? One thing it misses?"

Why it matters: Every prototype creates a feedback loop.
And every loop moves you closer to clarity. The habit here is not
building—it's learning to learn.

Fast-Track Hack: Create a Prototype Shelf—digital or physical.
Each drop builds momentum, and before long, you may find your
archive is driving insight you didn't expect.

Create the Conditions, Reap the Breakthroughs

Creative problem solving isn't a soft skill. It's a strategic lever. The Flow Design Matrix™ combines the structural precision of Design Thinking with the mental clarity and energy of peak engagement—unlocking a dynamic problem-solving model built for the demands of the modern era. This is your new operating system—where ambiguity becomes fuel, not friction.

Train daily. Share widely. Iterate constantly.

Up next: your Creative Problem Solving Toolkit—battle-tested templates to run breakthrough sessions, sharpen your creative edge, and lead teams into clarity faster.

Creative Problem Solving Workshop Toolkit

For Executive-Led Innovation Sessions

Overview

This toolkit equips executive leaders to run 60–90 minute sessions designed to:

- Engage teams in meaningful problem-solving
- Trigger flow and focus
- Apply design thinking without jargon
- Produce actionable outcomes, not just ideas

Use Cases

- Reframing a persistent business challenge
- Aligning on a customer pain point
- Creating strategic initiatives
- Jumpstarting innovation in siloed teams
- Fixing internal inefficiencies

Toolkit Components

1. Workshop Flow (Agenda)
2. Pre-Session Prep
3. Team Roles & Ground Rules
4. Facilitator Prompts & Scripts
5. Templates & Tools
6. Wrap-Up & Next Steps

Workshop Flow (60–90 Minutes)

Time	Phase	Goal
5 min	**Kickoff & Framing**	Define purpose & focus challenge
10 min	**Empathy Mapping**	Uncover pain points, user insights
15 min	**Problem Definition**	Frame a tight, actionable "How might we..."
20 min	**Rapid Ideation**	Generate high-volume ideas using constraints
10 min	**Idea Review & Vote**	Shortlist top ideas
15 min	**Prototype Sketching**	Visualize or rough out solutions
10 min	**Debrief & Action Plan**	Decide what to test or pitch

Pre-Session Prep (Leader's Checklist)

- ☐ Book a distraction-free space
- ☐ Set a clear, challenge-focused intention (e.g., "Reimagine our onboarding experience")
- ☐ Invite 4–8 diverse thinkers (cross-functional preferred)

☐ Print or share templates (see below)

☐ Prepare markers, sticky notes, whiteboards, or digital collaboration tools

Roles & Ground Rules

Roles:

- **Facilitator:** Guides the process (you or someone else)
- **Timekeeper:** Keeps momentum
- **Recorder:** Captures key insights, decisions, next steps

Ground Rules:

- Diverge before you converge
- Suspend judgment during ideation
- Quantity before quality
- Use "Yes, and..." mindset
- Assume best intent
- Document everything, no matter how rough

Facilitator Prompts & Scripts

Kickoff Prompt:

"Today, we're solving a challenge together—quickly and creatively. The goal isn't to debate or be perfect. It's to explore, test, and get messy in service of solving a real need."

Empathy Mapping Questions: Example(s)

Question	Example: New Hire Onboarding	Example: Digital Expense Reporting
Where are people getting stuck?	*Too much info on day one; systems access takes too long.*	*Employees unsure what counts as a reimbursable expense.*
What's frustrating or confusing about their experience?	*They don't know who to ask for help or where to start.*	*Concerning guidance from different departments.*
What workarounds are they using?	*Asking peers informally, creating personal checklists.*	*Saving receipts and submitting them all at once monthly.*

Problem Definition Prompt:

"Based on those pain points, let's define a 'How might we...' that we can solve today."

e.g., "How might we make onboarding feel energizing instead of overwhelming?"

Ideation Kickstart Prompts:

- "What would we do if we had no money?"
- "How would a 10-year-old solve this?"
- "What's the wildest possible approach?"

Prototype Prompt:

"Sketch or outline what this might look like—fast. Think MVP, not masterpiece."

Debrief Prompt:

"What's one next step we can take this week to test or explore this idea?"

Templates & Tools

(You can create these in Word, Google Docs, or Miro/Notion for teams)

Empathy Snapshot Template: Example(s)

Pain Point	User Quote	Frustration Level (1–10)	Workaround
Too much on day one	"I was drinking from a firehose."	8	Created their own checklist
Expense categories unclear	"I always ask my coworker what to file under."	6	Just submits it all at month-end

Problem Framing Sheet: Example(s)

Who is experiencing the issue?	What are they trying to do?	What's stopping them?	"How might we…" Statement
New hires in their first 30 days	Get oriented quickly and feel confident in their role	Overwhelming info, inconsistent onboarding experience	How might we make onboarding feel energizing instead of overwhelming?
Managers of remote teams	Build strong team connection and trust across time zones	Lack of informal touchpoints and awkward meeting dynamics	How might we help remote managers foster authentic connection more easily?

Rapid Idea Grid: Example(s)

Idea	Bold Factor	Ease of Test	Notes
Onboarding Scavenger Hunt with digital badges	High	Medium	Fun and gamified; test with one new hire group
Slack-integrated "Ask Me Anything" onboarding bot	Medium	High	Use existing Slack bot tools like Donut or Workflow Builder
Pre-paid expense cards with preset categories	High	Low	Requires finance/ legal buy-in—test with a limited group
"3-Field" Google Form for expense reporting	Low	High	Easy to build and deploy in one afternoon
Notion onboarding dashboard w/ intro videos & checklist	Medium	High	Can build in <2 hours and pilot with upcoming new hire cohort

Prototype Sketch Boxing: Example(s)

(Use blank boxes or slides for hand-drawing or roughing out ideas.)

Sketch Box A	Sketch Box B
Draw what the Notion onboarding dashboard might look like (modules, links, video blocks).	Draw layout of the 3-field expense Google Form (fields, submit button, upload receipt).

Action Plan Tracker: Example(s)

Next Step	Owner	By When	Support Needed
Build Notion dashboard prototype for onboarding	Alex (Design)	Friday	Video script from HR, access to Notion
Set up 3-question Google Form for expenses	Sam (Ops)	Wednesday	Finance to review questions
Test bot-based Slack onboarding with one team	Jordan (IT)	Next Tuesday	Buy-in from Team Lead
Schedule pilot with next new hire cohort	Maria (HR)	Next Monday	Coordination with hiring manager

Wrap-Up & Next Steps

- Choose 1–2 ideas to test
- Assign owners and timelines
- Schedule a 15-minute check-in for follow-up
- Capture what worked about the session
- Celebrate creative risk-taking—even if you didn't "solve" it

Want More Lift?

For longer sessions (half-day or more), you can add:

- Customer interviews or storyboards
- Competitive teardown exercises
- Lightning talks from internal experts
- Feedback rounds with external stakeholders

Turning Challenges into Breakthroughs

As a leader, your role is to create the conditions that allow your team to thrive in uncertainty. This toolkit isn't just a set of steps—it's a blueprint for unlocking your team's full creative potential. By embracing flow and design thinking, you're not just solving problems; you're building a culture of continuous innovation, adaptability, and collaboration.

Remember, great ideas don't just emerge from the right strategy—they come from the right environment, where focus, challenge, and trust can flourish. As you guide your team through these workshops, keep the following in mind:

- **Create space for risk:** Innovation happens when people feel safe to experiment without fear of failure.
- **Stay in the zone:** Foster an environment where focus and deep work are prioritized, allowing your team to access their best ideas.
- **Keep iterating:** The most successful solutions rarely come from a single idea. Encourage testing, feedback, and evolution.
- **Celebrate progress:** Whether the outcome is a breakthrough or an insightful lesson, acknowledge the value of every step toward solving the challenge.

Your leadership can catalyze breakthroughs that shape the future of your organization. By using this toolkit, you're not only solving today's problems—you're empowering your team to create the future, together.

Stay bold. Stay creative. And most importantly, keep your head in the game.

Part V:

The Future-Proof Executive

Technology is evolving fast. Human leadership must evolve faster.

AI, task automation, and ethical challenges are reshaping the leadership landscape. This section prepares you to lead responsibly in a rapidly evolving world—embracing innovation without losing the human touch. It's not just about keeping up; it's about shaping what's next.

A Story of Leadership in the Digital Age: InnovateTech's Journey into AI

The following story reflects the struggles many face in today's fast-paced, innovation-driven world. It's a tale of navigating challenges, balancing progress with ethics, and leading teams through uncertain terrain. While InnovateTech is a fictional company, the lessons from their journey mirror the challenges executives across industries encounter as they adapt to the digital age.

InnovateTech, a fast-growing tech company specializing in software solutions for healthcare, was facing a major crossroads. As the company expanded, its leaders realized that adopting Artificial Intelligence (AI) could significantly boost operational efficiency, improve patient outcomes, and stay ahead of the competition. However, they also knew that the ethical implications of AI—such as data privacy, algorithmic bias, and transparency—could not be overlooked. The leadership team, led by CEO Julia Martinez, decided to integrate AI into their business model while ensuring they adhered to the highest ethical standards.

The Challenge

InnovateTech was tasked with improving its healthcare management system, which collected and analyzed patient data to optimize treatment plans. AI could accelerate this process, making predictions about patient conditions more accurate, suggesting treatments, and even recommending preventive measures. But the idea of relying on AI in healthcare raised concerns among stakeholders, especially around data privacy and fairness.

Julia Martinez, a seasoned executive known for her ethical approach to business, knew that successful integration would require a careful balance between innovation and responsibility. She also recognized that her team needed to be aligned and engaged throughout the process, both technically and ethically. The decision was made to take a broad, inclusive approach to AI adoption—one that would integrate technology, human values, and rigorous oversight.

Leadership at the Helm

Julia understood that for AI to be integrated successfully, leadership had to play a vital role in shaping the narrative and direction of this shift. She began by assembling a cross-functional team that included not just data scientists and engineers, but also ethicists, legal experts, and representatives from various healthcare communities.

The first step was establishing a clear ethical framework for AI. Julia advocated for a focus on transparency, fairness, and accountability, ensuring that the company's AI solutions would be transparent in their decision-making processes and capable of being audited at any time. She emphasized that AI should never replace human judgment, but instead augment the expertise of healthcare professionals, with a focus on improving patient care.

Navigating Pitfalls

As InnovateTech began developing their AI models, they encountered several challenges. One of the first hurdles was the risk of bias in the algorithms. The training data used for the AI models was derived from historical healthcare data, which reflected past biases in treatment. Julia's team realized that if not properly addressed, these biases could perpetuate unfair treatment recommendations, leading to a higher probability of harmful consequences for certain patient groups.

Julia's influence played a pivotal role in guiding the company through this issue. She encouraged her team to adopt a "bias mitigation" approach—ensuring that the AI models were continually audited and adjusted to prevent negative outcomes. This involved collaborating with diverse healthcare professionals to ensure the models represented a wide range of patient needs and conditions. Julia also pushed for external audits by independent experts to maintain transparency and integrity throughout the process.

Another challenge was maintaining the privacy of sensitive patient data. Julia ensured that all AI applications complied with strict privacy standards and that patients were informed and gave consent before their data was used. She championed the development of advanced encryption techniques and data anonymization methods, ensuring that AI would enhance patient care without compromising privacy.

The Results

After months of rigorous testing, ethical considerations, and technical development, InnovateTech's AI system was deployed. The results were impressive. Healthcare providers using the system reported a significant increase in diagnostic accuracy, reduced patient readmissions, and better-tailored treatment plans. Patients experienced improved outcomes due to more personalized care recommendations, while healthcare professionals could rely on the AI tools to assist with decision-making.

But perhaps the most significant achievement was the recognition InnovateTech received for its commitment to ethical AI. The company became a model for others in the tech industry, receiving awards for innovation and responsible AI development. Julia's promotion of an ethical AI strategy not only enhanced InnovateTech's reputation but also helped establish a set of best practices for others to follow.

Leadership Lessons

The success of InnovateTech's ethical AI integration showcased the power of a strong, values-driven approach. Julia proved that ethical leadership—where responsibility, innovation, and progress are intertwined—could drive exceptional results. Her approach was to navigate the complexities of AI while fostering a culture of accountability and transparency.

Her approach was key to:

Assembling the Right Team: Julia ensured that AI development wasn't solely in the hands of technologists but involved ethicists, healthcare professionals, and legal advisors, creating a multi-faceted approach to AI integration.

Fostering Collaboration and Transparency: Julia's open communication and collaboration with external auditors and stakeholders built trust in the AI system, reassuring both healthcare providers and patients.

Championing Ethical Standards: Julia kept the ethical implications of AI at the forefront of decision-making, ensuring that the company's innovations were always aligned with its core values of fairness, accountability, and transparency.

In the end, InnovateTech's successful AI integration stemmed from an executive team that viewed innovation as a tool for societal good, not just profit. Julia's holistic and ethical approach paved the way for long-term success and set a new standard for responsible implementation and progress in the digital age.

What Julia modeled is possible for any leader who chooses to merge innovation with integrity. As you consider how her story resonates with your role, you'll find a clear pathway just ahead—a framework that allows you to act with both power and principle.

The AI-Ready Executive: Leading Through Technological Disruption

AI isn't just another tech trend—it's a tectonic shift. It's rewriting the rules of competition, compressing time limits for decision-making, and expanding what's possible in how we lead.

As a modern executive, your job is no longer just to guide people. You now have to guide systems—some of which 'think,' learn, and evolve on their own. That's a whole different game.

Reality Check: If your playbook doesn't include AI fluency, you're not future-proofing—you're falling behind. And your team knows it.

AI doesn't eliminate the need for leadership—it raises the bar. While the machines are optimizing, someone still must steer the mission, protect the values, and make the high-stakes calls. That someone is you.

But you can't do that well if you're still clinging to the old rules.

The Leadership Shift Has Already Begun

Here's what's changing:

Dimension	Traditional Leadership	AI-Augmented Leadership
Decision-Making	Experience-driven, reactive	Predictive, data-informed, proactive
Communication	One-way, periodic	Real-time, adaptive, insight-rich
Talent Management	Resume- and role-based	Skills, potential, and performance-signaled
Strategic Planning	Annual, fixed, assumption-heavy	Continuous, scenario-modeled, adaptive
Customer Understanding	Surveys, historical data	Real-time sentiment and behavior analysis
Risk Management	Gut instinct, basic modeling	Simulation-driven, anomaly detection, predictive alerts

Each of these shifts doesn't just make your business more efficient—it redefines your role as a leader. You're not just setting vision anymore. You're designing systems of intelligence. You're creating new capabilities that outpace the competition. And you're doing it while ensuring people stay at the center of it all.

What the Near Future Holds

In the next 2–5 years, executives will face challenges that would've sounded like science fiction a decade ago:

- AI managing AI: Algorithms that fine-tune other algorithms without human intervention. Who's accountable when it goes wrong?

- AI shaping culture: From automated performance feedback to AI-generated onboarding, the "tone" of leadership may soon come from bots. Are you shaping that tone—or letting it shape you?

- Decision velocity wars: Companies are racing not just to make better decisions, but to make them faster. The bottleneck? Human hesitation.

- Information inequality: Leaders who build AI fluency will compound insights. Those who don't will operate from a filtered version of reality.

Insight: The real question isn't whether AI will help you—it's whether you're ready to lead when speed and ambiguity hit full throttle.

Leadership Archetypes: Old vs. New

Outdated Archetype	What's Missing	AI-Ready Leader	What They Do Differently
The Gut-Driven Veteran	Intuition > Insight	The Augmented Strategist	Blends experience with machine foresight
The Charismatic Orator	Speech > Signal	The Real-Time Communicator	Uses data dashboards and generative AI to align messages instantly
The Hierarchical Hero	Control > Collaboration	The Networked Architect	Designs decentralized systems of decision-making
The Lone Visionary	Ego > Ethics	The Ethical Systems Thinker	Builds trust through transparency and accountability in AI systems

What This Looks Like in Action

Illustrative Scenario: Imagine a CTO at a global logistics firm who replaces static annual planning with dynamic, AI-powered forecasting that adjusts weekly to market conditions. The shift cuts decision latency by 20%, improves inventory precision, and empowers frontline teams to act in real time. In this scenario, the CEO attributes the company's resilience during a turbulent global supply chain crisis to this shift in approach—while competitors struggled to adapt.

Executive Reflection: In what areas are you still relying on experience and instinct—when smarter, faster inputs are available? More importantly, what's the cost of that hesitation?

Your Next Move

Great leaders don't wait for certainty. They build systems that reduce uncertainty faster than the competition.

- Don't outsource AI strategy to your tech team—partner with them.
- Don't pretend the status quo is safe—it's quietly becoming irrelevant.
- Don't wait to be "ready"—you get ready by engaging now.

Remember: You're not just leading a company. You're leading it through the most impactful technological shift of our lifetime. Learn fast. Act faster. *Stay human.*

The Human-AI Ethics Compass™: Ensuring Responsible AI Use

Coming into this new paradigm, it's clear that AI is fundamentally changing the rules of engagement. But while speed, prediction, and data can accelerate decisions, they can also amplify harm. The deeper your organization integrates AI, the more high-stakes your ethical responsibilities become. That's why we developed the Human-AI Ethics Compass™—to help executives translate values into consistent, high-stakes decisions under pressure.

The Human-AI Ethics Compass™ offers a directionally sound approach for integrating AI into decision-making with human values at the core. It's designed to help executives navigate with integrity, responsibility, and foresight.

The most visionary leaders are already asking not just, "Can we do this with AI?" but "Should we?" The pace of innovation doesn't excuse ethical shortcuts. It demands greater clarity, ownership, and courage from the top.

Tough Truth: If you don't lead the ethics conversation, someone else will—and it won't go in your favor.

The Human-AI Ethics Compass™: Six Ethical Anchors for AI Leadership

These principles provide a directional guide for leading with integrity in an AI-driven world—starting with transparency and ending with broader societal impact. These are not in arbitrary order—they follow a natural progression: visibility, ownership, equity, protection, oversight, and awareness of impact.

Transparency

Transparency means that the operations and decisions of an AI system can be understood, explained, and traced. It includes clarity about the data sources, the logic behind the algorithms, and the rationale behind each output or recommendation.

If you can't explain what your system is doing, you can't defend it—to regulators, clients, or the board. When AI makes critical decisions, stakeholders expect clear reasoning, not technical jargon. Demand explainability from internal teams and vendors alike. Push for tools like model cards, audit logs, and decision trees that allow you to audit the logic before problems arise.

Accountability

Accountability is knowing exactly who is responsible for the outcomes AI systems produce, whether those outcomes are positive or harmful. That responsibility applies not just to the design phase, but to how the system is deployed and acted upon.

When no one owns the result, everyone passes the blame. That's a culture killer. Assign executive sponsors for key initiatives and establish clear decision rights. Make it unequivocally understood: AI doesn't dilute responsibility—it concentrates it.

Fairness & Bias Mitigation

Fairness means ensuring your AI systems do not perpetuate or magnify discrimination—especially against historically marginalized groups. Bias mitigation requires proactively finding and fixing disparities across every stage of the AI lifecycle.

AI reflects the data it learns from, and that data is often full of human bias. If fairness isn't designed in from the start, injustice will be automated at scale. Define fairness explicitly for your business and make it measurable. Integrate bias audits and leverage open-source tools to identify disparate outcomes—before your system makes real-world decisions that can't be undone.

Privacy

Privacy in AI is about protecting sensitive personal and regulated data—during collection, storage, processing, and decision-making. This includes financial data, medical records, behavioral patterns, and more.

Data isn't just a resource—it's a responsibility. One breach, one misused dataset, and trust evaporates. Make privacy an executive-level conversation. Build processes that emphasize consent, data minimization, and real-time risk assessment. Ensure every system that touches customer data is held to the same standard you'd expect for your own.

Human Oversight

Human oversight ensures that people—not machines—retain the ability to monitor, intervene, and override AI decisions, especially in high-risk situations. It reinforces the role of human judgment where stakes are too high to automate completely.

AI can't grasp context, nuance, or moral weight. That's your job. Determine exactly where human review is required—whether that's in healthcare diagnostics, hiring decisions, or financial approvals. Make sure your systems know when to stop and let a human lead.

Societal and Reputational Impact

This principle considers how your AI systems affect not just your bottom line but the broader world—your customers, communities, and long-term brand.

What feels like innovation internally can be experienced as harm externally. Social backlash, regulatory scrutiny, or customer alienation can follow decisions that didn't anticipate their real-world ripple effects. Engage with outside perspectives early. Build in public interest thinking—not as a PR move, but as a strategic layer of risk management.

Operate with Intent

AI ethics isn't theoretical—it's operational. This is not about being perfect. It's about leading intentionally. You don't need to be an engineer, but you do need to lead like one: grounded in facts, unafraid to question assumptions, and bold enough to intervene before your company is featured in tomorrow's headline for the wrong reasons.

The Human-AI Ethics Compass™ reframes ethics not as the cost of innovation—but as the currency of trust. And trust is the most valuable asset you'll ever lead.

Intelligent AI Integration Strategy

Now that we've established the ethical foundation, the next step is putting AI to work—intelligently. Not every AI implementation fails because of bad code. Many fail because there was no clear plan for alignment, oversight, or scale. Others succeed technically but cause internal chaos or external damage because they rushed to deploy before understanding what they were really integrating.

This is where strategy meets responsibility. You can't duct-tape AI onto legacy systems and expect transformation. You need a deliberate, phased approach—one that aligns the power of AI with your company's values, capabilities, and risk tolerance.

Brutal Truth: Most "AI Innovations" are glorified pilot programs without long-term vision. If you don't lead this with intention, you're just playing with tech toys while your competitors build empires.

We recommend a four-phase model for intelligent, scalable AI integration. Each phase builds on the last, moving from exploration to enterprise-wide value:

Phase 1: Assess & Align

Before you build anything, you need clarity. What problem are you solving? Why AI? What would "good" look like?

This is where vision is most critical—and where many initiatives go off the rails. The focus isn't on throwing AI at inefficiencies—it's on targeting high-leverage opportunities that align with your strategic goals and core values.

Ask:

- Does this initiative solve a significant business problem or just chase a trend?
- Who benefits? Who might be harmed?
- Do we have the infrastructure, data quality, and people readiness to succeed?

Bring in legal, compliance, data teams, and frontline operators early. If your project can't pass the "alignment test" here, it has no business going forward.

Phase 2: Ethical Build

Now you begin to prototype and test—but ethics must stay front and center.

This phase is where the abstract values you committed to earlier become system design decisions. You'll need to embed fairness, privacy, and transparency into the build, not tack them on at the end.

Too many leaders hand this phase off to developers with little guidance. That's a mistake. The ethical architecture of your AI is shaped here—and once it's baked in, it's hard to change.

What to focus on:

- Bias testing: Are you using representative and clean data?
- Privacy protections: What sensitive data is being accessed? Is consent in place?

- Explainability: Can you explain the outputs to stakeholders and regulators?
- Governance checkpoints: Who reviews progress, and when?

This is where values become code. If you aren't involved, don't be surprised when you don't like the results.

Phase 3: Human Loop

You're not just building a system—you're designing a new kind of collaboration between people and machines.

This is the phase where many AI projects break trust—because they assume automation replaces judgment. But human oversight is not optional, especially in high-risk or customer-facing workflows.

Define:

- Where humans must approve, override, or guide decisions.
- The training required for teams interacting with AI outputs.
- How frontline employees escalate concerns or flag model errors.

This is a culture shift. Your teams must feel empowered, not replaced. And your customers must feel served, not surveilled. That's a leadership challenge, not a technical one.

Phase 4: Scale & Govern

This is where the AI strategy becomes enterprise-wide—and where true commitment is tested.

Scaling responsibly means putting systems in place to govern ongoing learning, functional drift, and new ethical risks. AI models evolve, and so must your oversight. Without governance, even a well-built system can become a liability.

Build frameworks for:

- Continuous monitoring and output auditing
- Version control and model documentation
- Clear escalation paths when AI goes off-script
- Retraining triggers and sunset criteria

More importantly, set the tone from the top: just because it works doesn't mean it should scale. Value alignment must be an ongoing filter, not a one-time check.

Executive Decision Framework

Decision Dimension	Key Questions	Executive Action
Strategic Fit	Does this initiative align with our long-term business goals?	Approve only if tied to measurable value and customer impact.
Ethical Soundness	Have we tested for bias, privacy, and fairness?	Require documentation and review from multidisciplinary teams.
Human Integration	Are human roles clearly defined and trained?	Codify oversight, review paths, and escalation protocols.
Governance & Scalability	Can we monitor, update, and govern this model at scale?	Approve scaling only if lifecycle governance is in place.

Beyond the Launch

AI strategy isn't about getting to launch—it's about staying in control after launch. The strongest leaders don't just deploy AI—they build systems of trust, visibility, and adaptability around it. That's how you go from pilot to platform, from hype to impact.

Real-World Applications: Leading with Purpose in AI Integration

As we move from theory to practice, it's important to see how leading companies are applying the AI integration strategies discussed earlier. The following real-world examples illustrate how organizations across industries are operationalizing AI with a clear focus on ethical considerations, human oversight, and strategic governance.

These case studies demonstrate the tangible benefits of embedding AI into business processes while maintaining a strong ethical framework, ensuring that AI solutions are both effective and responsible. By examining these examples, you'll gain insights into how to navigate the challenges and opportunities that AI presents in the modern business landscape.

JPMorgan Chase: Scaling AI with Human Oversight

JPMorgan Chase has integrated AI across its operations, with 200,000 employees utilizing a suite of Large Language Models (LLMs). These tools assist in tasks ranging from client interactions to legal documentation. The bank emphasizes that AI augments human work rather than replacing it, ensuring rigorous controls and data privacy. This approach highlights the importance of human oversight in AI deployment, aligning with the 'Human Loop' phase of the integration strategy.

Mattel: Leveraging AI for Product Feedback Analysis

Mattel collaborated with Google Cloud to analyze customer feedback on its Barbie Dreamhouse product using BigQuery AI tools. This initiative allowed Mattel to gain deeper insights into consumer preferences and improve product development. The project underscores the 'Assess & Align' phase, demonstrating how AI can be used to align product offerings with customer expectations.

Renault Group's Ampere: Ethical AI in Software Development

Renault's EV and software subsidiary, Ampere, employs an enterprise version of Gemini Code Assist to aid its development teams. This AI tool understands the company's codebase, standards, and conventions, facilitating efficient and ethical software development. The use of such tools aligns with the 'Ethical Build' phase, ensuring that AI integration adheres to established ethical standards.

Telstra: Joint Venture for AI Integration

Telstra, in partnership with Accenture, established a $700 million joint venture to incorporate AI across its operations. This initiative focuses on improving process efficiency and data utilization, with a strong emphasis on training Telstra's tech team. The strategy reflects the 'Scale & Govern' phase, highlighting the importance of structured governance in AI deployment.

GE: Enhancing Customer Support with AI

General Electric (GE) implemented AI to analyze support tickets, improving usability and optimizing resource allocation. This application of AI enhances decision-making processes and aligns with the 'Human Loop' phase by supporting human agents in customer service roles.

These case studies highlight the real-world impact of thoughtful AI integration. They show that when AI is deployed with a clear strategy, ethical guardrails, and robust human oversight, it can drive significant business value while fostering trust and accountability.

As you reflect on these examples, consider how your own organization can adopt similar strategies—whether you're starting with small-scale pilot programs or scaling up to enterprise-wide AI initiatives.

The key takeaway is that AI is not just a tool to optimize business operations, but a catalyst for innovation that requires careful leadership. By embedding responsible practices from the outset, you'll not only future-proof your organization but also ensure that AI serves to enhance both business outcomes and societal good.

Micro Habits: Daily AI Comfort-Building for Executives

Let's be honest—AI can feel like too much, too fast. Even the smartest executives fall into the trap of avoidance or leaning too heavily on specialists. But real comfort with AI is built the same way as fitness, communication, or strategy—through consistent reps, not just theory.

This isn't about becoming an AI engineer. It's about becoming a leader who speaks the language, knows the terrain, and feels confident asking the right questions. Daily familiarity builds strategic fluency. The goal is progress, not perfection.

Straight Talk: You wouldn't step into a high-stakes negotiation after reading one article on influence. So why assume you can lead an AI-driven organization with no reps under your belt? Micro-habits beat macro-theories every time.

Four Daily Habits to Build AI Stamina

These aren't just suggestions—they're deliberate reps designed to hardwire AI awareness into your daily operating rhythm. Done consistently, they shift AI from a buzzword to a trusted asset.

Start with a 10-Minute AI Briefing

Skim one high-quality, curated AI newsletter each day. Prioritize sources that cut through the noise and frame developments in terms that matter to business leaders. This primes your brain for pattern recognition, sparks creative applications, and keeps you from falling behind.

Examples: The Rundown, TLDR AI, Ben's Bites

Test One New AI Tool Per Week

Pick a day each week to try a new AI-powered tool relevant to your workflow—writing, meetings, research, planning. Don't just explore it, apply it. See what clicks, what feels clunky, and how your team could benefit. This turns curiosity into capability.

Suggestions: ChatGPT, Notion AI, Fireflies.ai, Claude, Perplexity, GrammarlyGO, Otter.ai

Facilitate a Weekly Human-AI Discussion

Host a 10–15 minute team conversation once a week. Frame it around one prompt: "Where could AI help—or harm—our work?" This builds psychological safety around experimentation and creates space for creative, ethical thinking.

Bonus Tip: Rotate who brings the example or use a breaking news story as a starting point.

Use AI for Decision Prep—Not Just Output

Before your next big decision, use AI to surface perspectives you might miss. Try using prompt-based assistants to simulate stakeholder responses, analyze tradeoffs, or uncover hidden biases in your assumptions. This builds pattern awareness and sharpens your strategic edge.

Take up the Challenge

What's the smallest AI habit you could commit to this week that moves you one step closer to fluency? Pick one. Write it down. Do it daily for 14 days. Then reassess.

Master the Mindset, Not the Model

This AI playbook isn't about mastering machine learning models—it's about mastering the mindset required to lead in a world shaped by them.

AI doesn't change the fundamentals of leadership. It raises the stakes. It compresses timelines, amplifies decisions, and accelerates consequences. And in doing so, it calls for a new kind of executive—one who is adaptable, inquisitive, ethically grounded, and comfortable using tools they may not fully understand at the code level but deeply understand at the strategic level.

You don't need to control the algorithm. You need to guide the outcomes. That starts with building daily fluency, nurturing your team's AI literacy, and showing up as the kind of leader who learns in public—and leads with integrity.

Because in the age of AI, the most human leader wins.

Part VI:

Closing the Leadership Loop

Growth isn't a phase—it's a mindset.

This section brings together the core reflections that tie your evolution together. You'll revisit the big takeaways, reflect on the ongoing nature of leadership development, and hear a final word from behind the scenes.

Leadership doesn't stop at the last page—this is your call to continue, to connect, and to lead forward with purpose.

Key Takeaways from the Book

This book is more than just theory—it's a call to action. You've explored a new leadership model that fuses performance, ethics, and innovation. What follows isn't a summary—it's a distillation of the mindset, habits, and skills you must integrate to lead in today's high-stakes environment. These are your non-negotiables for thriving in the digital age.

A New Standard for Leadership:

In today's digital landscape, effective leadership goes beyond strategy. It demands integration of mental discipline, physical resilience, ethical awareness, and technological fluency. The old playbook doesn't cut it anymore.

Master the Inner Game:

Focus, clarity, and emotional regulation aren't optional—they're prerequisites. Mindfulness and mental training build the foundation for decisive action under pressure.

Lead with Strength and Stamina:

Your body is your engine. Leaders who dial in sleep, nutrition, and movement don't just last longer—they lead better. Health is a performance multiplier.

Communicate with Purpose, Lead with Grit:

In a world of noise, clear communication and unshakable resilience are your edge. Influence isn't about volume—it's about precision, presence, and emotional connection.

Innovate on Demand:
Creative problem-solving and flow states aren't just "nice to have." They're your unfair advantage. Leaders who cultivate innovation mindsets ignite teams and drive breakthrough results.

Lead Ethically in the Age of AI:
AI is here. Your job is to integrate it wisely—enhancing human potential without losing the human touch. Ethics, oversight, and responsibility aren't add-ons; they're the framework.

Never Stop Evolving:
Leadership isn't a title. It's a practice. The best never coast—they adapt, grow, and lead forward, always ready for what's next.

If you take nothing else from this book, remember this: leading is a dynamic practice. These takeaways are not just ideas to consider; they are principles to live by. Start small, act daily, and evolve constantly. The future isn't waiting for perfect leaders—it's calling for committed ones. Lead forward.

You've gathered tools, stories, and strategies—but the real transformation begins when these ideas become part of who you are. As you reflect, you may already feel a shift, a new lens through which you're seeing your leadership. That's not accidental. It's the beginning of your evolution.

The Imperative of Ongoing Leadership Development

Leadership isn't a finish line—it's a discipline that requires constant calibration. The pace of change in business, innovation, and culture has surpassed the traditional models we were taught to rely on. What worked yesterday won't take you into tomorrow.

Executives who thrive in this new world do three things consistently:

They grow: They adopt a mindset of continuous learning and adaptability.

They integrate: They align physical health, mental clarity, and emotional intelligence to operate at full capacity.

They lead with integrity: They embrace innovation—especially AI—but never at the cost of ethics or human connection.

Command-and-control thinking is obsolete. Reactive problem-solving isn't enough. Modern leadership is inclusive, forward-looking, and grounded in a clear personal compass.

If you want to stay relevant, you must evolve. Develop new capabilities. Rebuild old habits. Cultivate resilience, creativity, and clarity—not just for yourself, but for the people who rely on your guidance.

In this era, the best leaders aren't just strategic. They're human-centric, tech-aware, and fiercely committed to growth. That's the edge. That's the expectation. And that's the mission.

Leadership Reinvented: The Origin Story of Xecutive 2.0

This Isn't a Story About Perfection.

It's a story about pressure, persistence, and purpose.

My path to leadership wasn't handed to me—it was forged through a unique blend of military values, technical precision, and hard-earned human insight. I've faced the kinds of tests that don't show up on resumes: the moments when you're overextended, under-resourced, and still expected to lead with clarity. It's in those moments—when everything's on the line—that I discovered what leadership really is.

Built from Battle-Tested Values

I come from a family of service and sacrifice. One uncle parachuted into Normandy and took a bullet through the shoulder on the way down. Another fought in the Battle of the Bulge. My father served in the Reserves. These weren't just stories—they were lessons.

I learned early that leadership isn't about showing up when it's easy. It's about standing firm when it's hard. Resilience wasn't an abstract value. It was our way of life.

Our family's commitment to leadership through adversity runs even deeper—back to ancestors who fought to preserve the Union during the Civil War. And in my own lifetime, I witnessed history firsthand at the fall of the Berlin Wall—a moment when the world didn't change through conquest, but through the undeniable force of human courage, unity, and hope.

Those experiences shaped how I see leadership: not as authority, not as title, but as the ability to step forward when it matters most.

From Operator to Leader

I began my career solving complex technical problems under pressure as a network engineer. But the deeper I went, the clearer it became: the biggest challenges weren't in the code. They were in the communication. They were in the leadership.

The leap no one prepares you for isn't technical. It's human. I moved into program management, then executive roles. The more responsibility I took on, the more undeniable it became: technical expertise is only half the game. The real leap—the one that defines you—is learning how to lead people.

That's when everything changed.

Why Xecutive 2.0 Exists

When I started helping others navigate that leap, I saw brilliant minds burning out. High performers struggling to delegate. Technologists hitting a wall when they stepped into elevated roles.

So, I made it my mission to bridge that gap—to guide the transition from operator to leader, from reactive to strategic, from driven to truly impactful.

That's how Xecutive 2.0 was born.

It's not a coaching program. It's not a productivity hack. It's a full-spectrum ecosystem system for executives ready to rise into the future without losing themselves.

Built on Three Core Beliefs

Truth in Leadership – Real transformation starts when you face the truth, no matter how uncomfortable, and use it as your catalyst for growth—individually, organizationally, and culturally.

Work-Life Integrity – Burnout isn't a badge of honor. True performance comes from doing what matters, with focus and energy, without sacrificing your ambition—or your life.

Adaptability & Innovation – Today's challenges don't wait for you to catch up. You must stay ahead by embracing change, integrating technology thoughtfully, and leading from the front.

The Invitation

Xecutive 2.0 was built for today's executive—the leader navigating complexity, driving innovation, and striving to stay fully present at home.

If that's you, you're not alone. And no—you don't need to become someone else to lead powerfully.

You need a system, a mindset, and a community designed for the real world you lead in. That's what Xecutive 2.0 delivers.

This is your invitation to evolve. To become the leader who acts with clarity, executes with conviction, and inspires through genuine human connection.

Whether you're stepping into your first executive role or redefining leadership in your second act, we're here to walk that path with you.

Step Into the Room

You've already started the journey. Now step into the room where leaders like you refine their edge—and often find exactly what they didn't know they needed.

Growth doesn't happen in isolation—it accelerates in the right environment. And that's exactly what the Xecutive 2.0 Community is built for:

A space for those of us serious about growth, resilience, and leading with purpose.

Inside, you'll get direct access to high-level discussions, practical tools, and real accountability.

No fluff. No ego. Just honest, relentless progress—with others who demand the same of themselves.

You Took the First Step. Now Here's Your Reward.

You're not on the sidelines. You're already in the arena—and this next move might be the catalyst that changes your entire trajectory.

If you're ready to go deeper, this is your invitation to join the Xecutive 2.0 community—where high-performance leadership becomes a lived reality.

Scan the QR code below to unlock
your reader-exclusive reward.

25% off your first month inside the community.

Use code: X2UNLOCK at checkout.

This is where frameworks meet feedback.
Where peers push you forward.
And where your next level
becomes non-negotiable.

Lead Boldly,
John 'Lex' Robinson
Lead | Empower | Xecute

Afterword:

Lead What's Next

You've reached the end of this book—but this isn't the finish. It's your launchpad.

What you've read isn't a rulebook. It's an adaptive blueprint for creating the future. Every principle here—mental mastery, physical optimization, ethical AI, creative problem-solving—exists to help you lead with clarity, confidence, and impact.

But remember: None of it works unless you act. Leadership isn't built on information alone. It's built on execution, intention, and the courage to lead with purpose.

Take what resonates. Test it. Apply it. Make it your own. The true measure of leadership lies in your ability to adapt, innovate, and act with strength, empathy, and conviction.

This new era isn't just about technology. It's about integrating technology in ways that amplify human potential and foster flourishing. The future belongs to those who lead with vision, integrity, and relentless commitment to growth.

Now, go lead—not just to succeed, but to shape a future where humans, not machines, are at the center of everything we do.

Acknowledgments

This book reflects not just my work, but the wisdom, support, and encouragement of many people who shaped the journey behind *Xecutive 2.0.*

To my clients—thank you for your courage, your trust, and your relentless drive to grow. Your breakthroughs inspired many of the ideas in this book, and your stories gave them life.

To the leaders I've had the privilege to serve alongside—both in the military and the corporate world—you helped forge the principles of resilience, accountability, and decisive leadership that run through these pages. I am especially grateful to those who challenged me to lead with more empathy, and not just precision.

To my mentors and peers in technology, coaching, and strategy—thank you for pushing the boundaries with me. Your influence helped shape the frameworks, sharpen the questions, and remind me of the human core inside the digital noise.

To my family, who taught me the meaning of strength, humility, and legacy—thank you for keeping me grounded and driven by purpose.

To the readers—thank you for choosing to become something more than what the world expects. This book is a challenge and an invitation. I'm honored to be part of your journey.

Let's build what's next—together.

— Lex

About the Author

John 'Lex' Robinson is a leadership strategist, performance coach, and veteran technologist with over three decades of experience driving transformation across Fortune 500 companies, military operations, and high-performance executive teams.

A former soldier turned technology executive, Lex has built data centers, led global programs, and developed the next generation of tech leaders from the ground up. His unique blend of military discipline, technical depth, and human-centered coaching makes him a trusted advisor to executives navigating the complexity of the digital age.

As founder of **The Viros Group** and creator of the **X2OS™ Xecutive Operating System**, Lex empowers ambitious professionals to sharpen their minds, strengthen their resilience, and unlock their full potential. His coaching integrates neuroscience, emotional intelligence, and flow state science to help leaders rise—not by working harder, but by leading smarter.

Lex holds a certification in Generative AI Leadership and Strategy and is the author of *Beyond Limits: Harnessing Flow for Peak Performance*. He brings truth, empathy, and exacting standards to every engagement—challenging us to evolve in a world that won't wait.

When he's not coaching or building new frameworks, you'll find him reading about future tech, training on the trail, or guiding emerging leaders through their toughest challenges with a blend of hard-earned wisdom and relentless belief in human potential.

Connect with Lex and Join the Movement at The Viros Group (thevirosgroup.com)

Appendix:

Tools, Plans, and Resources for Implementation

Ideas are only as powerful as the actions they inspire.

This appendix gives you the practical tools to embed everything you've learned. From a 90-day leadership development plan to frameworks, book recommendations, and innovative research, this is your resource hub for continued growth.

Leadership Development Roadmap: From Insight to Execution

This roadmap is your guide from initial awareness to sustained growth. It aligns with the key pillars of this book—human connection, cognitive mastery, ethical innovation, and peak performance—and helps you put them into action. Whether you're stepping into leadership for the first time or seeking to elevate your current role, the roadmap shows you where you are and how to level up. Consider it a companion to your 90-Day Action Plan, offering strategic direction for long-term growth.

How to Use This Roadmap

There is no single path to becoming a high-impact executive. Use this roadmap to identify where you currently operate and which areas to strengthen. You may be strong in one domain and a beginner in another. Start where the urgency or resonance is highest, then expand.

Stage 1: Awareness & Audit

"You can't change what you're not aware of."

At this stage, you begin recognizing the habits, beliefs, and behaviors that limit your leadership skills. You audit your current style, energy levels, communication habits, and your relationship with technology. This is where honesty meets curiosity.

Key Actions:

- Complete a self-assessment (using tools in this book)
- Identify patterns of avoidance, burnout, or misalignment
- Define what kind of leader you want to become

Stage 2: Activation

"Insight without action is entertainment."

Here, you take your most urgent insights and begin applying them to daily life. You experiment with new habits—mindfulness, better communication, focused decision-making, ethical AI use—and observe what sticks.

Key Actions:

- Begin the 90-Day Action Plan
- Track one or two key behaviors daily
- Establish simple routines to support flow, recovery, and presence

Stage 3: Integration

"Consistency builds credibility—with yourself and others."

This is where systems start replacing willpower. Your new behaviors become part of your identity. You integrate high-impact rituals, emotional regulation, and cognitive enhancements into your rhythm.

Key Actions:

- Build flow sessions into your weekly calendar
- Use feedback loops from your team to adjust
- Align your physical health, mental clarity, and emotional capacity with your professional demands

Stage 4: Amplification

"Now you teach it, coach it, scale it."

You're no longer just improving yourself—you're elevating your team, culture, and impact. You begin mentoring others, building AI-augmented processes that reflect ethical values, and leading from a place of vision, not just execution.

Key Actions:

- Create systems and rituals for your team
- Use your story to inspire change
- Measure outcomes tied to well-being, culture, and strategic outcomes

Leadership Development Roadmap

Stage	Focus Area	Key Behaviors	Tools/Support
Awareness	Audit & Clarity	Self-assessment, journaling, honest feedback loops	Leadership audit template, self-reflection guide
Activation	Daily Habit Formation	Begin 90-Day Plan, single-tasking, EQ practice, mindful decision-making	Daily trackers, Fast-Track Hacks
Integration	Identity & Systems	Flow rituals, energy management, AI ethics framework, feedback implementation	Flow Design Toolkit, wearable data, coaching
Amplification	Team & Culture Leadership	Mentorship, visionary thinking, culture scaling, ethical AI implementation	Leadership systems map, storytelling framework

Your Leadership Journey Is Just Beginning

This roadmap isn't a checklist—it's a compass. Success isn't defined by a destination—it's driven by purposeful evolution. As you move through these stages, you'll find yourself revisiting earlier phases with new insight and deeper capacity. Use this framework to track your growth, realign when needed, and accelerate your impact. The world doesn't need more reactive managers—it needs resilient, creative, human-centered visionaries. That's who you're becoming.

If you've made it this far, something's already shifting. You've seen the future of leadership—now here's how to make it real. This isn't about big leaps. It's about stacking small wins until excellence becomes automatic.

90-Day Leadership Development Action Plan

Welcome to your Development Action Plan. This framework is designed to help you apply the principles from the book to your daily practices. Over the next 90 days, you'll focus on key areas such as cognitive enhancement, emotional intelligence, resilience, and integrating innovation and ethics into your leadership style. This plan bridges the gap from theory to action, ensuring the insights you've gained translate into tangible results.

How to Use This Plan

This 90-day plan is not meant to be tackled all at once. Instead, choose *one area* that resonated most deeply with you while reading — whether it's mastering your mindset, enhancing emotional intelligence, or leading with ethical AI. Start there. Go deep. Build consistency.

Once you've built momentum in one area, you can cycle back to explore others. Sustainable transformation happens through focused, intentional practice — not scattered effort.

Mindset & Cognitive Enhancement

Goal: Cultivate a growth mindset and enhance mental clarity for better decision-making.

Action Steps:

- **Day 1–10:** Implement a daily mindfulness practice (e.g., meditation, deep breathing) to improve focus. Start with 5 minutes per day and increase gradually.
- **Day 11–20:** Dedicate 15 minutes every morning to brain exercises (e.g., puzzles, problem-solving) that enhance cognitive flexibility and creativity.
- **Day 21–30:** Begin journaling to track your mental and emotional states. Reflect on how cognitive enhancement techniques are impacting your focus and clarity.
- **Day 31–60:** Practice mindfulness during meetings or critical decision-making moments. Take 3 deep breaths before responding to stressful situations.
- **Day 61–90:** Apply mindfulness in high-stakes environments (e.g., presentations, tough conversations). Track improvements in your ability to stay calm and make clear decisions.

Resources:

- Mindfulness apps: Headspace, Calm
- Cognitive training: Lumosity, Peak

Emotional Intelligence (EQ)

Goal: Enhance your emotional intelligence to improve your resilience and interpersonal relationships.

Action Steps:

- **Day 1–10:** Focus on active listening during meetings. Avoid interrupting and summarize what others say to ensure understanding.
- **Day 11–20:** Identify your own emotional triggers. Note when you feel stressed or reactive and reflect on the underlying emotion.
- **Day 21–30:** Implement empathy exercises. In 1:1 meetings, ask team members about their feelings and concerns—and listen without judgment.
- **Day 31–60:** During challenging interactions, pause before responding. Identify your emotional state and reframe it to respond thoughtfully.
- **Day 61–90:** Continue practicing empathy and regulation in high-pressure moments. Reflect on outcomes and how your EQ influenced team dynamics.

Resources:

- Book: *Emotional Intelligence 2.0* by Travis Bradberry
- Journaling techniques to track emotional responses

Physical Health & Biohacking

Goal: Improve physical health to boost cognitive function, energy, and stamina.

Action Steps:

- **Day 1–10:** Establish a sleep routine. Set a consistent bedtime and wake-up time. Aim for at least 7 hours of quality sleep each night.

- **Day 11–20:** Focus on nutrition. Incorporate more brain-boosting foods (e.g., leafy greens, omega-3s, lean proteins) into your diet.
- **Day 21–30:** Begin a regular exercise regimen. Aim for 30 minutes of activity, 3–4 times a week (both aerobic and strength-based).
- **Day 31–60:** Try biohacking practices (e.g., intermittent fasting, cold showers, or wearables to track your health data).
- **Day 61–90:** Continue optimizing sleep, exercise, and nutrition. Track how these affect your energy, focus, and output.

Resources:

- Book: *The Bulletproof Diet* by Dave Asprey
- Apps: *Sleep Cycle*, MyFitnessPal
- Wearables: *Oura Ring*, Whoop

Flow State Mastery

Goal: Learn to enter and maintain flow states to improve creativity, problem-solving, and decision-making under pressure.

Action Steps:

- **Day 1–10:** Identify one task per day for total focus (e.g., deep work). Eliminate distractions and block dedicated time.
- **Day 11–20:** Practice "single-tasking." Avoid multitasking to protect your attention span.
- **Day 21–30:** Incorporate light movement into your day (e.g., walking, stretching) to improve blood flow and clarity.
- **Day 31–60:** Develop "pre-flow rituals" like music, breathing exercises, or inspirational reading before deep work.

- **Day 61–90:** Use techniques such as deep breathing, and visualization during high-stakes decisions to enhance clarity and composure.

Resources:

- Book: *Flow* by Mihaly Csikszentmihalyi
- Music: *Brain.fm*
- Apps: *Focus@Will*

Leading with Ethical AI

Goal: Understand how to integrate AI into decision-making while maintaining ethical standards.

Action Steps:

- **Day 1–10:** Learn the basics of AI and its ethical implications. Read articles or take an intro course.
- **Day 11–20:** Audit your organization's AI use. Identify opportunities for ethical improvement or new use cases.
- **Day 21–30:** Apply an ethics framework to your decisions. Ask: How can AI support humans without replacing or biasing them?
- **Day 31–60:** Engage with AI experts. Invite dialogue with your team to surface ethical concerns and ideas.
- **Day 61–90:** Develop or refine an AI strategy that prioritizes transparency, fairness, and accountability. Review impact regularly.

Resources:

- Online Course: *AI for Everyone* by Andrew Ng (Coursera)
- Article: *The Ethics of Artificial Intelligence* by Nick Bostrom

Final Reflection

At the end of 90 days, pause and reflect:

- How has your mindset, emotional intelligence, physical energy, or ethical approach to technology evolved?
- What new habits have stuck?
- Where do you still want to grow?

This plan isn't meant to be a one-time sprint — it's a foundation. Keep revisiting, revising, and integrating what you learn. As you do, you'll unlock deeper levels of clarity, connection, and capacity.

Frameworks for Implementing Leadership Concepts

Leadership today demands more than just theoretical knowledge—it requires actionable strategies that integrate into your daily life. The frameworks in this section are designed to provide you with a clear, structured approach to development, making it easy for you to apply powerful principles to your work and life. These frameworks are not just theoretical—they come with practical tools and templates to ensure you can track your progress and implement them with confidence.

Each framework represents a core aspect of modern leadership and provides step-by-step guidance to update your approach. Whether you're looking to improve your resilience, foster creativity, or implement ethical AI practices, these frameworks will serve as your guide to elevating your skills. With the tools provided, you can begin immediately to integrate these strategies into your routine, building habits that enhance your abilities and drive results.

How to Use These Frameworks

These frameworks are designed to be explored one at a time, allowing you to dive deeply into each area for maximum impact. Start by selecting the framework that resonates most with your current needs—whether it's building resilience, optimizing flow, or ensuring ethical AI practices. Focus your energy on that framework, implementing its strategies consistently until you see measurable growth.

Once you've built a solid foundation in one area, you can move on to the next framework, gradually expanding your capabilities. Remember, true success is not about tackling everything at once, but about cultivating mastery through intentional, focused action over time.

The Mind-Body Leadership Framework

Integrating mental, physical, emotional, and technological mastery into daily practices, ensuring a comprehensive approach to leadership.

In today's landscape, we often talk about managing teams, driving results, and meeting targets. But what about the leader themselves? A well-rounded leader understands that the foundation of success starts with mastering their own mind, body, and emotions. According to research in both neuroscience and performance psychology, high-level leadership requires balance across all aspects of life, not just one or two. When mental clarity, emotional resilience, physical health, and high-tech literacy are aligned, we can operate at our highest potential, influencing others in more impactful ways.

This framework will guide you through the integration of key practices that elevate each of these domains. You'll learn how to optimize your thinking, physical abilities, emotional intelligence, and high-tech adaptability—all of which will empower you to lead with greater clarity, focus, and effectiveness.

Framework Overview:

- **Mental Mastery:** Cognitive enhancement, critical thinking, mindfulness, decision-making.
- **Physical Mastery:** Health optimization, physical fitness, energy management.
- **Emotional Mastery:** Emotional intelligence (EQ), empathy, self-regulation, resilience.
- **Technological Mastery:** AI ethics, digital literacy, leveraging technology for effective decision-making.

Steps to Implement:

1. **Start with Reflection:** Begin by assessing where you are in each of the four areas (mental, physical, emotional, and technological). Identify strengths and areas for improvement.
2. **Set Priorities:** Choose one area to focus on first, based on what will have the greatest immediate impact on your effectiveness.
3. **Create a Routine:** Develop a daily practice for each mastery area. For example, engage in 10 minutes of mindfulness for mental mastery or 30 minutes of exercise for physical mastery.
4. **Monitor Progress:** Use the provided Mastery Goal Tracker to check in on your progress weekly and adjust as needed.
5. **Expand Gradually:** Once you feel confident in one area, begin adding practices from the other domains to your routine, creating a holistic development plan.

Mastery Goal Tracker

Purpose: To set and track measurable goals in each of the four mastery areas of the Mind-Body Framework.

How to Use:

- In the "Goal" column, define a specific outcome for each mastery area.
- Outline 2–3 clear action steps to move toward that goal.
- Use the "Progress Tracker" column to check off daily or weekly progress.
- Review at the end of each week to assess alignment and adjust as needed.

Mastery Area	Goal	Action Steps	Progress Tracker
Mental Mastery	Increase cognitive flexibility	10 minutes of mindfulness daily	[ ] Day 1 [ ] Day 2...
Physical Mastery	Improve physical fitness	Exercise 3x/ week (cardio & strength)	[ ] Week 1 [ ] Week 2...
Emotional Mastery	Enhance emotional intelligence	Practice active listening every day	[ ] Day 1 [ ] Day 2...
Technological Mastery	Learn a new tech tool each month	Complete an online course in AI ethics	[ ] Month 1 [ ] Month 2...

The Resilient Leadership Framework

Building resilience by focusing on mindset, emotional intelligence, and adaptable strategies.

The modern environment is full of uncertainty, rapid changes, and unexpected challenges. Research in personal development consistently shows that resilience is one of the most critical qualities for sustained success. Resilient leaders are not just those who endure challenging times—they're the ones who thrive despite them. A resilient leader can pivot when needed, manage stress without losing focus, and inspire teams to persevere even in adversity.

This framework will help you develop resilience by enhancing your mindset, emotional awareness, and adaptability. You'll learn how to leverage challenges for growth and maintain emotional balance, so you can not only survive but thrive in the most demanding situations.

Framework Overview:

- **Growth Mindset:** See challenges as opportunities for growth.
- **Emotional Awareness:** Recognize and regulate emotions during difficult moments.
- **Adaptive Leadership:** Be flexible in the face of change, focusing on long-term solutions.

Steps to Implement:

1. **Reframe Challenges:** Shift your perspective on obstacles—view them as opportunities to learn and grow, rather than threats.
2. **Build Emotional Awareness:** Practice daily mindfulness or journaling to better understand and regulate your emotions.
3. **Strengthen Your Support System:** Cultivate relationships with mentors, peers, and team members to provide emotional and strategic support during tough times.

4. **Take Adaptive Actions:** When faced with a challenge, use a structured decision-making process to find flexible solutions and adjust your approach as needed.
5. **Track Resilience Growth:** Regularly assess your resilience through reflection and feedback to gauge improvement.

Resilience Action Plan

Purpose: To build resilience through deliberate action in the emotional, mental, and relational domains.

How to Use:

- Identify one action under each "Resilience Focus" category that supports your capacity.
- Set a deadline or cadence for execution.
- Use the "Outcome" column to define what success looks like and reflect weekly.
- Revisit and revise monthly based on performance and feedback.

Resilience Focus	Action Plan	Deadline	Outcome
Emotional Reflection	Journal daily on emotional triggers	Daily	Increased self-awareness
Stress Management	Practice deep breathing or time blocking	Weekly	Reduced stress levels
Continuous Learning	Take a course on leadership adaptability	3 Months	Strengthened adaptability
Support Systems	Connect weekly with mentor or peer group	Weekly	Greater emotional and strategic support
Mindset Conditioning	Reframe setbacks as growth opportunities	Ongoing	Improved resilience response

The Flow Leadership Framework

Optimizing effort by leveraging flow states to enhance focus, creativity, and problem-solving.

Achieving a state of deep immersion isn't just for athletes or artists—it's a critical tool for leaders. This is the state where a person is so fully engaged in their work that they lose track of time and experience optimal productivity. According to the research of Mihaly Csikszentmihalyi, this state is linked to higher levels of creativity, and well-being. For leaders, this mental state enables the ability to think clearly, make better decisions, and inspire innovative solutions.

This framework will guide you through the process of creating the right conditions for flow within yourself and your team. You'll learn how to manage distractions, find the perfect balance between challenge and skill, and keep goals clear foster sustained excellence.

Framework Overview:

- **Clarity of Goals:** Ensure that tasks and projects have clear, measurable outcomes.
- **Challenge-Skill Balance:** Engage in tasks that stretch your skills without overwhelming you.
- **Autonomy and Focus:** Minimize distractions to allow deep concentration.

Steps to Implement:

1. **Set Clear Goals:** Define exactly what success looks like for each project or task.
2. **Find the Right Challenge:** Choose tasks that align with your current skill level but still offer enough challenge to promote growth.

3. **Eliminate Distractions:** Establish "deep work" periods where distractions are minimized, allowing you to focus solely on the task at hand.
4. **Engage the Team:** Help your team members understand how to achieve flow by setting clear expectations and fostering an environment of trust and autonomy.
5. **Reflect on Flow Experiences:** After each high-focus session, take time to reflect on what conditions allowed you to enter flow, and apply these insights to future work.

Flow State Checklist

Purpose: To ensure the conditions for flow are in place before entering deep work or creative tasks.

How to Use:

- Review each condition before a focused work session.
- Check the box that reflects your current readiness status.
- Adjust your environment or task framing to meet any unmet conditions.
- After the session, reflect on what worked and what to improve next time.

Condition for Flow	Checklist Item	Status
Clarity of Goals	Are goals clearly defined and measurable?	[] Not Started [] In Progress [] Completed
Challenge-Skill Balance	Do tasks match but slightly stretch current capabilities?	[] Not Started [] In Progress [] Completed
Minimized Distractions	Are external distractions and multitasking minimized?	[] Not Started [] In Progress [] Completed
Deep Work Environment	Is there a designated time and space for deep work?	[] Not Started [] In Progress [] Completed
Post-Flow Reflection	Are lessons from flow states captured and reviewed regularly?	[] Not Started [] In Progress [] Completed

The Ethical Leadership & AI Framework

Ensuring responsible stewardship by integrating AI ethically into decision-making and organizational culture.

As AI continues to play an increasing role in business, leaders must be equipped to use it responsibly. Ethical issues surrounding AI include bias, privacy, and transparency. Those who fail to address these concerns risk damaging trust and alienating both employees and customers. Ethical AI use is not just a moral obligation but also a business necessity. A leader who understands and implements ethical AI practices builds long-term trust, ensures fair decision-making, and sets a standard for responsible innovation.

This framework will guide you through the core principles of ethical AI use, ensuring that you can leverage this powerful tool without compromising your integrity or the trust of your team. You'll explore practical strategies for integrating AI while maintaining transparency, accountability, and fairness.

Framework Overview:

- **Transparency:** Keep AI systems and decisions clear and understandable to all stakeholders.
- **Accountability:** Ensure that humans remain accountable for the outcomes of AI-driven decisions.
- **Fairness:** Implement AI tools that are free from bias and discriminatory practices.

Steps to Implement:

1. **Review Ethical Standards:** Familiarize yourself with the key ethical guidelines around AI and leadership.
2. **Implement Transparent Practices:** Ensure that any AI tools or algorithms are clearly explained to your team and customers and maintain transparency in decision-making.
3. **Test for Bias:** Regularly audit AI systems for fairness and remove any bias in data sets or algorithms.
4. **Establish Human Oversight:** Ensure that humans are accountable for all AI-driven decisions.
5. **Educate the Team:** Help your team understand the ethical implications of AI and encourage ongoing education in this area.

Ethical AI Use Guidelines

Purpose: To operationalize ethical AI principles into daily decisions, product reviews, and team practices.

How to Use:

- For each principle, define a specific action your team or organization will take.

- Assign responsible individuals or teams to each action.
- Use the "Implementation Status" column to track progress.
- Review quarterly to update practices based on new insights, tools, or regulations.

Ethical AI Principle	Action Steps to Integrate	Implementation Status
Transparency	Define how AI decisions will be communicated to stakeholders	[] Not Started [] In Progress [] Completed
Accountability	Ensure AI systems include clear human oversight	[] Not Started [] In Progress [] Completed
Fairness	Audit data sets and algorithms for bias before and during use	[] Not Started [] In Progress [] Completed
Education & Awareness	Train your team on ethical AI use and emerging issues	[] Not Started [] In Progress [] Completed
Continuous Monitoring	Set up regular reviews of AI behavior and ethical implications	[] Not Started [] In Progress [] Completed

Closing Thoughts

These frameworks and tools are designed to provide a clear and actionable path to implement leadership concepts in your daily life. Whether you are focusing on building resilience, creating flow conditions, or ensuring ethical AI integration, these frameworks serve as a comprehensive guide to development. The accompanying tools make it easy to track your progress, ensuring that each action is aligned with your goals.

Leadership is a continuous journey, not a destination. By using these frameworks and tracking your progress with the provided tools, you'll be equipped to lead with purpose, adaptability, and ethical integrity in today's fast-changing world.

References, Further Reading & Research for the Xecutive Leader

To lead effectively in an era of complexity, high performance, and digital acceleration, today's Xecutive must be grounded in proven science, ethical insight, and timeless leadership principles. The following curated works—ranging from academic research to foundational leadership texts—offer deeper context and practical frameworks behind the strategies in this book.

Foundational Reads

- Bennis, W. G. (2009). *On becoming a leader* (Rev. ed.). Basic Books.
- Brown, B. (2018). *Dare to lead: Brave work. Tough conversations. Whole hearts.* Random House.
- Clear, J. (2018). *Atomic habits: An easy & proven way to build good habits & break bad ones.* Avery.
- Cialdini, R. B. (2006). *Influence: The psychology of persuasion* (Rev. ed.). Harper Business.
- Csikszentmihalyi, M. (1990). *Flow: The psychology of optimal experience.* Harper & Row.
- Duhigg, C. (2012). *The power of habit: Why we do what we do in life and business.* Random House.
- Goleman, D. (1995). *Emotional intelligence: Why it can matter more than IQ.* Bantam Books.
- Goleman, D., Boyatzis, R., & McKee, A. (2013). *Primal leadership: Unleashing the power of emotional intelligence* (Rev. ed.). Harvard Business Review Press.

- Holiday, R. (2014). *The obstacle is the way: The timeless art of turning trials into triumph.* Portfolio.

- Kabat-Zinn, J. (1994). *Wherever you go, there you are: Mindfulness meditation in everyday life.* Hyperion.

- Kotler, S., & Wheal, J. (2017). *Stealing fire: How Silicon Valley, the Navy SEALs, and maverick scientists are revolutionizing the way we live and work.* Dey Street Books.

- McChesney, C., Covey, S., & Huling, J. (2012). *The 4 disciplines of execution: Achieving your wildly important goals.* Free Press.

- McChrystal, S. A., Collins, T., Silverman, D., & Fussell, C. (2015). *Team of teams: New rules of engagement for a complex world.* Portfolio.

- Newport, C. (2016). *Deep work: Rules for focused success in a distracted world.* Grand Central Publishing.

- Sinek, S. (2009). *Start with why: How great leaders inspire everyone to take action.* Portfolio.

- Tegmark, M. (2017). *Life 3.0: Being human in the age of Artificial Intelligence.* Alfred A. Knopf.

- Walker, M. P. (2017). *Why we sleep: Unlocking the power of sleep and dreams.* Scribner.

- Whitten, A. (2020). *Eat for energy: How to beat fatigue, supercharge your mitochondria, and unlock all-day energy.* Whitten Group Press.

Scientific & Strategic Sources

Neuroplasticity & Cognitive Performance

- Ooi, R. W. G. (2025). *From neurons to organisations: Awakening regenerative leadership through neuroplasticity, AI, and integrative consciousness* (Version 2) [Preprint]. Preprints.org. https://doi.org/10.20944/preprints202501.0743.v2

- Costa, R., & Wilson, B. (2022). The emergence of neuroleadership in the knowledge economy. *Behavioral Sciences,* 12(9), 320. https://www.mdpi.com/2673-8392/4/3/71

- Di Stefano, G., Gino, F., Pisano, G. P., & Staats, B. R. (2014). Learning by thinking: How reflection aids performance. *Harvard Business School Working Paper Series.* https://www.researchgate.net/publication/272302319_Learning_by_Thinking_How_Reflection_Aids_Performance

Emotional Intelligence & Leadership Resilience

- Côté, S. (2022). Emotional intelligence, leadership, and work teams: A literature review. *Heliyon*, 9(1), e13764. https://www.sciencedirect.com/science/article/pii/S2405844023075643

- Rao, G. P., Koneru, A., Nebhineni, N., & Mishra, K. K. (2024). Developing resilience and harnessing emotional intelligence. *Indian Journal of Psychiatry*, 66(Suppl 2), S255–S261. https://doi.org/10.4103/indianjpsychiatry.indianjpsychiatry_601_23

Biohacking, Sleep, & Health Optimization

- Harvard T.H. Chan School of Public Health. (2022). Healthy eating for a healthy brain. *The Nutrition Source.* https://nutritionsource.hsph.harvard.edu/healthy-eating-plate/

- Huberman, A. (2021). Focus toolkit: Tools to improve your focus & concentration. *Huberman Lab.* https://www.hubermanlab.com/episode/focus-toolkit-tools-to-improve-your-focus-and-concentration

- National Sleep Foundation. (2023). The effects of insufficient sleep and adequate sleep on cognitive performance. *Sleep Health*, 9(1), 100–107. https://www.sleephealthjournal.org/article/S2352-7218(23)00293-0/abstract

- Smith, J. (2018). Enhancing health leadership performance using neurotherapy. *Journal of Applied Neuroscience*, 12(2), 89–101. https://pubmed.ncbi.nlm.nih.gov/29717646/

Systems Thinking, Leadership Psychology & Communication

- Mathew, P. (2023). Neuroscience and servant leadership: Underpinnings and implications for practice. In M. B. Green, R. R. Spears, & L. C. Spears (Eds.), *The Palgrave Handbook of Servant Leadership* (pp. 1573–1595). Springer International Publishing. https://doi.org/10.1007/978-3-031-01323-2_95

- National Institute on Aging. (n.d.). Cognitive and emotional health project: The healthy brain. *U.S. Department of Health and Human Services.* https://www.nia.nih.gov/research/dn/cognitive-and-emotional-health-project-healthy-brain

AI Ethics & Human-Centered Strategy

- Google AI. (2020). AI principles. *Google Responsible AI.* https://ai.google/principles/

- IBM Research. (2018). AI Fairness 360: An extensible toolkit for detecting and mitigating algorithmic bias. https://research.ibm.com/publications/ai-fairness-360-an-extensible-toolkit-for-detecting-and-mitigating-algorithmic-bias

- Microsoft. (2021). The building blocks of Microsoft's responsible AI program. *Microsoft AI Blog.* https://blogs.microsoft.com/on-the-issues/2021/01/19/microsoft-responsible-ai-program/

Where to Find These Resources

Most of the books listed above are available in hardcover, paperback, eBook, and audiobook formats via major retailers such as Amazon, Audible, and Barnes & Noble. Many of the scientific articles and reports can be accessed through:

- Google Scholar
- PubMed
- ResearchGate
- University databases or public libraries with academic access

If you're looking to explore further, we also recommend subscribing to trusted newsletters like Harvard Business Review, MIT Sloan Management Review, or The European Business Review to stay current on leadership science, innovation, and human-centered strategy.